Special Agent Charli

SPECIAL AGENT CHARLI

Mimi Barbour

Sarna Publishing

Contents

Special Agent Charli

Undercover FBI

Book #6
by
NYT & USA Today, best-selling author,
Mimi Barbour

~*~*~

*The only man she wants in her life is her old Gramps,
and all he wants is a great-grandchild.*

Special Agent Charli Madison can't get a break.
After the stress of her last horrific assignment, all

she wants is to spend time vacationing with her Gramps in Fort Lauderdale, a city they both love. Plans go awry, and she's forced into witness protection, guarding a teenage girl who's the only person able to identify a notorious killer.

To make matters worse, she has to accept the womanizing local FLPD Major as her fictitious fiancé and her backup on the dangerous mission.

Heaven knows, she doesn't deserve this mess...

Blake Sebastian is tired of his role as lover for the women who hang around him in droves. Problem is – he doesn't trust any of them with his heart, never mind with his future.

When pushed, he admits to the curly-headed, disapproving FBI agent under his jurisdiction, a man can get sick of so much sugar. Every so often, he needs a little sour to offset that much sweetness.

Charli was *not* impressed.

Dedication

My father, the man we all called Poppa John, was my hero. Plain and simple! I adored the man as a child, a young girl, a married woman and most of all as a senior who truly understood the battles against age he overcame to stay sweet and kind until the day he passed.

He loved to make people laugh, said their smiles gave him joy... and hope.

One time, my son asked him the secret of being a good person, and his answer still rings true – *be human.*

We all miss him terribly, and the only way I could bear losing him was to write him into this book as my favorite character of all time. (And just so you know, most of the anecdotes told in this book were based on the truth.)

He'll be remembered every time we see a yellow begonia, hear the song "Big, Bad John", and see the wonderful stain glass memories he left behind.

He was... and will always be... my special hero.

Praise for the Undercover FBI Series

"Can't wait to read more by this author. This was the first book I read by this author so my expectations weren't too much, but they should have been. I really enjoyed this book. I can't wait to read more of her books. I even joined her newsletter." ~ *reviewed by SusieQ*

"In my opinion, the Special Agent series by Mimi Barbour just keeps getting better and better. I loved this story, the humor, the characters and the plot...especially the things I didn't see coming. Wonderfully entertaining read!" ~ *reviewed by Anne C*

"Love Mimi Barbour, love her books. When you can read a book that within just a few words, you are brought right into the book. You feel, taste, see everything going on. Great story lines. Fantastic characters, fantastic plots, story lines like real life both honest folk and of crooks. Humor that will have you giggling then full on belly laugh. You may even shed a tear or two at love. You will also have visit from other Las Vegas cops from the Vegas series. All in all Mimi never disappoints, I loved the book and highly recommend." (Special Agent Francesca – Book #1 – Undercover FBI) ~ *reviewed by Shirleen*

Also author of...

Most of Mimi's books can be found FREE on Kindle Unlimited!!

~*~*~*~

The Vicarage Bench Series
— Spirit Travel at its Best! —
She's Me (Book 1)
He's Her (Book 2)
We're One (Book 3)
Vicarage Bench Anthology (Book 4 – Books 1-3)
Together Again (Book 5)
Together for Christmas (Book 6)
Together Always (Book 7)

***

Angels with Attitude Series
— Angels Playing Cupid! —
The Angels with Attitudes Anthology (Books 1-3)
My Cheeky Angel (Book 1)
His Devious Angel (Book 2)
Loveable Christmas Angel (Book 3)
A Wonderful Life (Book 4 to be released in Dec 2018)

***

Elvis Series
— Make an Elvis Song a Book! —
She's Not You (Book 1)

Love Me Tender (Book 2)

***

Vegas Series
— Action–Packed Thrillers! —
Vegas Series – Complete Boxed Set
Partners (Book 1)
Roll the Dice (Book 2)
Vegas Shuffle (Book 3)
High Stakes Gamble (Book 4)
Spin the Wheel (Book 5)
Let it Ride (Book 6)

***

Undercover FBI Series
— Popular & Compelling! —
Special Agent Francesca (Book 1)
Special Agent Finnegan (Book 2)
Special Agent Maximilian (Book 3)
Special Agent Kandice (Book 4)
Special Agent Booker (Book 5)
Special Agent Charli (Book 6)

***

Holiday Heartwarmers Trilogy
— Truly a Christmas favorite! —
Holiday Heartwarmers Series
Please Keep Me (Book 1)
Snow Pup (Book 2)
Find Me a Home (Book 3)
Frosty the Snowman (Book 4)
Love of my Life (Book 5)

***

Mob Tracker Series
— She's unstoppable! —
Sweet Retaliation (Book #1)
Sweet Justice (Book #2)
Sweet Resolution (Book #3
Sweet Endings – (Book #4)
Sweet Faith (Book #5)
Sweet Leni (Book #6 – released in Fall 2018)

***

Other Titles
I'm No Angel
Hotshot Cowboy
Big Girls Don't Cry
Christmas Runaway
The Surrogate's Secret
Mimi's Mix (Box Set)
'Tis the Season (Box Set)
Hearts, Flowers & Romance (Box Set)
Red Hot Divas (Box Set)
A Touch of Passion (Multi-author Box Set)
Love, Christmas (Multi-author Box Set)
Unforgettable Romances (Multi-author Box
Set)
Kiss Me, Thrill Me (Multi-author Box Set)
Sweet and Sassy (Multi-author Box Set)
Unforgettable Heroes (Multi-author Box Set)
Sweet Heat (Multi-author Box Set)
Unforgettable Christmas (Multi-author Box
Set)
A Christmas She'll Remember (Multi-author

Box Set)
Snowflakes and Christmas Kisses (Multi-author Box Set)
Unforgettable Valentine (Multi-author Box Set)
A Valentine She'll Remember (Multi-author Box Set)
Unforgettable Suspense (Multi-author Box Set)
Unforgettable Danger (Multi-author Box Set)
Unforgettable Trouble (Multi-author Box Set)
Unforgettable Weddings (Multi-author Box Set)
A Wedding She'll Remember (Multi-author Box Set)
Enchanted Romances (Multi-author Box Set)
Sweet and Sassy Brides (Multi-author Box Set)
Love, Christmas 2 (Multi-author Box Set)

***

All Mimi's books can be found on her Amazon Author Page:
http://bit.ly/MimiBarbourAmazon
OR
Website: http://mimibarbour.com

Chapter One

Relief filled Alicia Shoal. Her foster parents, Bud and Margo White, and their loser friends finally ran out of beer in the apartment and decided to move their loud party to a local bar. Without their drunken noise, she'd have a chance to finally settle the three little ones they'd dumped on her to babysit.

She'd tried to calm the smallest boy, but three-year-old Buddy Junior, the White's own kid, refused to share her attention.

A handful to say the least, a grumpy, dissatisfied child, he demanded constant care every moment he was awake. Thankfully, he too drifted off and that left her with the two-year-old toddler. Being the sweetest of the lot, she just needed a bit of a cuddle to settle down and close her eyes.

Breathing a sigh of relief, Alicia tiptoed from the bedroom, stretched and went to spray air freshener to clear away the distinct odor from the weed the adults had shared earlier. Then she cleared away the beer cans and empty snack dishes scattered all over the front room and kitchen.

The gluttons didn't leave any for her, but then they never did. After an hour of tidying, even her foster mother, slacker Margo, shouldn't find anything to bitch about. Alicia knew from experience, overcoming that hurdle took a lot of patience. When Margo was hungover, she pressed buttons and Alicia had to ignore a lot of crap.

Pushing back never paid off, she'd learned that lesson after the last three foster families. This time, she'd swallow the shit, keep her cool and wait and plan for her day of freedom.

She slid her fingers through her thick hair in the front and pushed the straight, black strands away from her neck and let them flow down her back. Being half Chinese, her black hair was a symbol of her heritage as much as her slightly almond-shaped dark brown eyes.

When she was younger, many others in the orphanage would tease her, make her aware of their differences. As she grew older, her slim Asian body became a real plus, and she stopped letting the slurs bother her.

Snagging the almost empty bag of pretzels and sneaking a coke from the bunch in the fridge, she headed for the sitting room to kick off her shoes and maybe get some homework done.

Her ninth grade math teacher was a stickler about the work she assigned and would phone the parents personally if her students didn't hand it in on time.

Earlier in the year, Margo had been called about Alicia, and she'd cut off Alicia's access to her stupid TV for a month by unplugging it and sticking it in their storage locker in the basement.

Considering this was her only form of entertainment, even though the dumb appliance was old, murky and small, she relied on having it for nights like tonight when she'd be expected to stay awake until the early hours of the morning. That's when everyone would come stumbling in drunk and disorderly to pick up their kids, and in some cases they wouldn't even bother until the next day.

Alicia lowered the bright lights to a dull roar rather than the full-on glare overhead that Bud liked. She hated feeling like a fish in a backlit bowl for all the neighbors to see.

The big windows across the front of their twentieth-floor Seattle apartment, in the middle of a bunch of other similar buildings, gave her the creeps. It made her feel like a target for some pathetic loser with no life and only a set of binoculars for entertainment.

She noticed that Bud, her foster father – and that moniker was a joke – had left his binoculars out. Usually, he'd lock them in the cabinet.

She sauntered over to pick them up, and as a lark, checked the dials so she could set them back as close to where they had been. Then she adjusted the lenses and leaning against the back of the sofa, she started to scan the buildings like she'd see Bud and Margo do all the time.

First, she looked to see if the older woman who lived in the building directly across was still up and watching TV. Bud had nicknamed her the "slouch on the couch" because most of the time that's where she'd be found. Sure enough, there she was tonight, apparently sound asleep, or if the booze bottle on the floor was any indication, she'd passed out.

Moving on, Alicia saw that the lights were dimmed in many of the windows but the building across from her, a floor lower, suddenly glowed. Attracted to the light, she focused there and her breath caught in her throat.

She watched a large male figure enter the scene. With a gun held firmly, he skulked around the apartment threateningly, hidden from the blonde woman who'd just turned on the light.

Moving without a care in the world, the beauty took two more steps and would be crowding his space any second.

Beautiful, in a silky kimono, long hair streaming over her shoulders, rubbing lotion on her hands, she sauntered slowly to face a monster she didn't know waited.

Alicia found herself whimpering. *Stop! Please!* Without intending to, she'd lifted her hand to wave frantically, to catch the other's attention. Gurgled screams, straining to be released, sent shockwaves throughout her system. Numerous nerve endings in her head lit, shooting adrenalin to all her alarm centers. She fought to gather her scattered thoughts.

What should she do? What *could* she do? She pranced in place – a majorette in a parade waiting for the music.

The prowler began to move, like a cat stalking his prey. This kept Alicia glued to the scene. With tension unleased, a voice inside her began to warn, to shriek... to pray.

God, Lady, can't you feel him waiting? Run, escape!

The binoculars became heavy, burdensome. She had a death hold on them. Clutched in her sweating hands, they didn't waver, though it took a herculean effort to keep them in place.

Still Alicia couldn't put them down – couldn't stop watching. Mesmerized by the horror, she had a sudden urge to pee and at the same time to run.

She did neither.

She watched.

The minute the woman stepped through the doorway, the lurker caught her by surprise. A punch in the face sent her flying across the room. He followed, lifted the gun and pointed it at the cowering woman now on her knees... begging.

Whatever he said, the woman knew her pleas were in vain. She stiffened. Before Alicia could take a second breath, she saw a small flash of light.

The bullet struck the victim's forehead, and the body flew backward in a sprawl against the couch. Only a small, dark hole in her head was visible. That tiny destructive stain symbolized the beautiful woman's departed soul and it all took place in just a split second.

Now, Alicia screamed.

As if the thin screeching sounds, ringing with terror, reached across the compound to the other building, the gunman turned and looked directly at her. Like a living entity, her fear must have drawn him, called to him and his instinct attached itself to that wire-like thread.

Whatever the reason, his gun was now pointed in her direction. His evil grin of accomplishment subsided, and his eyes zeroed in on her. His expressions changed swiftly from anger to warning then ended in pure determination. He would come for her. She knew it like she knew she couldn't stop him.

Dropping the binoculars, her heart pumping so hard she thought she'd faint, Alicia slid to the floor and cowered, squeaky whimpers escaping and ramping up her terror.

Hardly able to breathe, she dared another peek and saw the lights were now off across the way. It made her crawl to the wall where the switches for her place were located by the outside door.

"Oh my God, oh my God... help me." Urges to run, get away, hide clamored in her brain. She wrenched open the door and then stopped dead. What about the babies? How could she leave them?

She needed to call 911. But what would Bud and Margo say? They'd be totally pissed if she brought the law to their place, considering the recreational drugs that Bud always hid around the apartment.

Suddenly, she remembered a lifeline, an FBI agent, Carolina Madison, who lived down the hall. If Alicia sought her help, she'd have to do something... wouldn't she? A murder took place, she saw it. Carolina would have no choice but to believe Alicia after they found the body.

Not hesitating, though her knees gave out so she had to crawl the last few feet, Alicia banged on the door and begged, "Carolina Madison? Please help me. Oh God, help me."

Chapter Two

One week earlier:

Blake Sebastian had a hard time believing his career had come so far. In the past, he'd served in the Tactical Impact Unit, on the SWAT Team, and in the Fort Lauderdale Criminal Investigations Division, became a Sergeant, and eventually became certified as a defensive tactics and firearms instructor, among other things. After a few more steps up the ladder, he now occupied a position as Major of the Support Service Bureau. And it had all happened overnight.

Where had the time gone? He'd hit his mid-thirties and owned a lovely house he'd bought for a song when prices were low during the recession. He'd filled it with expensive boy-toys, a nice wardrobe and modern furniture. And he drove a very fast Jeep.

Was he any different than most his age? Maybe... He'd made the final payment on his student loans just that morning. And rather than feeling the overwhelming relief he'd thought would accompany his accomplishment, he'd experienced a sad reaction so unlike his norm.

Maybe it was Officer Cowan proudly showing off the baby pictures he and his wife had taken of their new daughter? They'd even gotten their year-old retriever puppy to preen for them beside the infant. The photos were cute. The kid was cute.

So what?

Shaking off the unexpected gloom, he fiddled with his pen, enjoying the few minutes of solitude he'd stolen from an otherwise hectic shift. Psychoanalyzing his minor depression, he faced the problem.

It's simple. He missed the day-to-day activities of a Sergeant. The on-the-street interactions with his men, and the people they served. As one of the bosses who managed to stay involved with most of the cases, he still craved more action.

A huge list of messages stared at him, creating distaste and a gloomy reaction so unlike his usual carefree nature. He split them into piles and noticed three numbers waiting for him to return their calls – from three starved-for-love women hoping to hear from their occasional lover.

Admitting that refuge in the arms of pretty women lightened the sadness fostered by the many atrocities that passed across his desk every day, he grinned when he read the names. All were gorgeous, two were rich and none were married.

He made no excuses, had no wife to cheat on, and he never fooled around with married women. Everyone needed a way to deal, and he'd found his drug of choice at the age of thirteen.

It happened when a set of twins five years his senior invited him to their apartment on the floor above where he'd lived with his parents. They'd educated him on the intricacies of satisfying every female fantasy they'd ever had.

His schooling had proven effective. He'd never understood how other females instinctively sensed his expertise, but they did. And he'd never suffered from a lack of attention from the ladies.

What they offered, he gladly accepted, making sure they never walked away without a smile on their faces and affection in their hearts. Intuitive, as soon as their eyes began to sparkle with more than the mild affection he'd shown them, he'd set them straight, his explanation copyrighted.

The line was drawn at long-term relationships, and he always warned his victims not to get too involved, too emotional. He loved the single life as much as he liked sharing many nights with various sex partners.

No more – no less.

His phone rang, disturbing his quiet time. A niggling feeling struck, making him hesitate. *What the hell?* The hair on his neck and arms performed like it did when he faced danger.

Somehow, he knew this call was going to change everything. Should he answer it? Feeling suddenly silly, his hand reached but hesitated before he lifted the receiver.

Chapter Three

Carolina Madison, Special Agent with the Seattle Drug Enforcement Agency finally had a night to relax and pack. With her major cases organized, paperwork completed, and her suitcases zipped, she had everything ready, waiting for her upcoming trip.

She'd spent the better part of the afternoon with her old gramps, the person who'd raised her, her mentor, her hero, the only man she'd ever loved wholeheartedly.

He'd been particularly sassy this day, teasing her about her plans for the future and telling her he'd never get to rock a great-grandbaby if she didn't fix her skewered attitude toward the noble males of the world.

"Noble? You should have seen what I recently witnessed Poppa John. Trust me; it isn't particularly honorable when men slink around like sick dogs selling drugs they know will ruin people's lives. Or their *male* bosses who care only about raking in the millions so they can buy yet another diamond earring or toy they don't need."

"Those folks aren't the ones I'm talking about and you know it. Charli, you gotta loosen up, kiddo. Men scare easily, and when you get that dogged look and your eyes fill with ice, it terrifies them."

Laughing at the visual, Carolina asked, "Pops, how do you know what I look like when I'm on the job?" She stopped her massage of his shoulders and bent to peer into his lined face. His one good eye, still brown, stared her down, while the bluish blind eye seemed to have sight, though she knew differently.

"'Cause that's your permanent expression when you talk about your work, so I'm assuming you probably walk around all day at the office looking like you just swallowed a squishy bug. And, I've seen you mad. Remember the time I warned you that the old woman down the hall was breaking into my place and stealing my stuff? I saw the look you got."

"Yeah, that was because I thought you meant she'd stolen your property, not some silly old medicated cream."

"Hey, that is my property. And it's not just any old *medicated cream*," he sneered the words. "It was my expensive B.C. Bud Rub you order for me online. I shouldn't have bragged about how well it worked on my knees or felt sorry for her and given the crazy old woman a sample."

Keeping her face straight, Carolina remembered how she'd tried to talk him out of his idea that some senior lady from down the hall had broken into his apartment, snuck into his fridge and helped herself to his cream. It had made no sense.

"I know you didn't believe me, but you sure changed your mind when she woke you up last weekend. I'm glad we'd guzzled too much wine at the restaurant next door, and you couldn't drive home. You spent the night here and caught her red-handed, right? Not so smart now, are we little girl? See, this old guy's still got it. And, I saw your expression when you turned on the light and caught her... colder than a witch's tit."

"Quit with the expressions, you brat. I wasn't being mean, just upset. I knew without your hearing aids, you couldn't hear anyone breaking in. It made me wonder how often she'd taken advantage of you."

"That never happened, kiddo. When she tried, I fought her off." Seeing her shocked expression, eyes twinkling merrily, he'd laughed loud and long.

Giggling again over his cheekiness, she let go of the memory.

Relaxed in her oldest, gray sweat pants with the word *sexy* written in bright pink over the butt cheeks – a gift from her goofy grandfather – paired with a t-shirt from Quantico, thick socks in rose-colored fluff and her red curls tied up in a mess over her head, she felt like a teenager.

Just that day, she'd finished writing up the intel on her latest undercover drug case, organized all the paperwork, and had handed the huge file in to her superiors.

Happily accepting their praise during the debriefing, she'd finally unwound when they'd agreed she should take time off. Drastically in need of a break, Carolina knew her limitations. They'd been reached weeks ago.

Infiltrating a gang of known felons, getting them to trust her enough to let her carry some of their precious cargo had taken perseverance and smarts. She'd lived on the edge; becoming a criminal in every way to fit in had taken its toll.

Starting at the Mexican port of entry, where they collected their drugs from their cartel associates, they taught her the Points of Entry and the avenues of delivery used to transport the cocaine to their hideaway in Seattle.

That knowledge had been a huge boost in helping her set up the sting. She'd led the taskforce to them, finally shutting down those corridors and charging two of the biggest drug lords in the city of Seattle.

Understandably, the adrenalin she'd lived on for the last three months had worn off, leaving her drained, quick to anger, and too jumpy by far.

And in the end, they'd moved in and taken the gang down in a shootout she'd never envisioned. Maintaining her cool with heavy doses of headache medication and sporadic, brief, but delightful, visits with her gramps had reached its pinnacle. She was done.

But that was over, she was home and wanted to forget those horrific moments. Last night, for nine hours she'd been out for the count with only a cup of milky hot chocolate and an open window as sedatives to help her sleep.

Home was the west coast of Washington State where they suffered from continuous rain for months, and she was tired of it. Her parents, both deceased from a horrific car accident on a slick road when she was a very young girl, had once rented them a house in Fort Lauderdale with a swimming pool and a full backyard of luxurious living.

The memories they'd made were still precious to this day. They'd taken Poppa John along with them, and his dunking her in the pool and making her play catch, and the constant hugs and teasing still ranked as some of her favorite recollections.

During that vacation, her gramps and mom had taught her how to make her favorite food, Perogies. They'd made a shitload and stuffed those dumplings with everything from potatoes and cheese to blueberries. God, she missed those days when they'd shared a home.

Left with only her weekly visits at the retirement home – affectionately known as the lodge – taking him on daytrips for lunches and shopping, movies and very short hikes, Carolina decided that her recent abandonment issues were stupid. He didn't want to live with her and give up all his activities with his peers who lived at the same old-age facility. Her guilt was misplaced.

There, he bowled, played a crazy kind of sit-down hockey, danced at the weekly happy hours and teased the ladies so that they babied the heck out of him. The caregivers adored the old coot, almost as much as she did. Even though she'd have loved to have him live with her, she accepted he'd have spent too many lonely hours waiting for her to come home. And that would be unthinkable.

Starting tomorrow, she had a month's vacation and meant to spoil herself with every costly treat she could think of. After her spinster aunt's will had been probated many years earlier, she'd come out with a cool million, both her and her parents. Since their money had eventually passed on to their only child, she'd have no financial worries. Invested properly, it would give her a nice home one day and a very good retirement.

In the meantime, deciding she'd need periodic spoiling, she'd left a slush account on the side to pay for a few wonderful vacations over the next several years. Her gramps had urged her to go, spend the money and have a good time. *Charli, my beautiful girl, let your gorgeous curly hair down, get pregnant, enjoy... ahh life.*

Ha! He did have a way with words. When she'd pointed out she didn't have a husband, he'd come back with a shocker.

"So what? Nowadays, you don't need a spouse to have a kid. Not if you don't want one."

She laughed again, her memories delightful. One thing she did agree with, she'd never needed a time-out more.

Once again, the southeastern coast of Florida called to her, and she'd made all the arrangements to vacation in Fort Lauderdale. She'd even found a lovely home to rent in a nice area with an oceanfront view and didn't care about it being too large for one person.

She'd invited her gramps to come for a visit once she got settled, which he'd happily accepted, and all his paraphernalia would soon fill up the place. He never heard of travelling light.

Unable to face a lot of vacationing research after the months she'd gone through, she'd fallen back on their favorite city from previous stays. As a get-away from the rigors of a life constantly on the edge, it suited her perfectly. The urban location, perfect for a sun-lover, held everything she could want. Trendy restaurants, wonderful shopping and vistas of ocean beauty close by would fill the heart of any person in need of cleansing dark memories.

Heading to the bathroom to turn on the hot

water in her spa tub and add the Japanese Cherry Blossoms bath soap that smelled delicious, she sauntered toward the hallway, calling out, "Alexa – turn on – *Man, I Feel Like a Woman* by Shania Twain."

In a few seconds the music poured from the Amazon Echo thingy her gramps had given her that year for Christmas. Skipping to the beat of her favorite song, careful not to spill a drop of her expensive, spicy-smelling, fruity-tasting Shiraz, wiggling and dancing while she moved, she hummed along with Shania.

As she neared the front door, all hell broke loose.

Someone banged for attention, and the ruckus stopped her in her tracks. Clear enough to grab her attention, female screams for help filtered through the solid wood.

Adrenalin surges simmering just below the surface from her last job kicked into high gear. Quickly putting her sloshed drink on the floor and retrieving her weapon from the hidden drawer where she stored it when she was at home, she readied herself and checked the peephole. Observing the distressed person on the other side, she breathed deeply and stuck her rioting curls behind her ears.

"*Alexa – turn off.*"

Chapter Four

Once she'd realized the threat looked to be female, hysterical and just a teenager, Carolina whipped open the door. "Stop that." She held the gun at her side and used her other hand to point at the girl's twisted features. "Stop screaming. Get in here."

Helping the girl into her place, she checked the corridor. "It's okay folks, she's with me. I'm Agent Carolina Madison, FBI." She shut and locked the door, and placed the gun behind her back in the waistband of her pants. Turning to the cowering girl, she grunted, "This better be good. Acting like a complete moron, screaming, upsetting everyone in the place. What possessed you?"

The quivering girl shouted; panic evident, "He's coming to kill me."

"Calm down." Carolina took the teen's wildly jerking hands in hers and held them in front of her, giving them a shake. "He who?"

As she listened, she automatically registered certain details about the slender teen's appearance. Her black hair worn long and straggly, moisture-filled brown eyes widened by fear, and the Chinese features, that showed a promise of beauty, stood out the most.

Voice again rising, hysteria the cause, the girl clarified, "The same man who killed the woman in the opposite apartment building."

Stunned by her reply, Carolina's radar slipped into operational mode. "A man killed a woman in the opposite apartment? How the hell do you know that?"

"I watched. He caught me. His evil expression through Bud's binoculars warned that he saw me. And he'll come. He knows where I live." Terror-filled, shaking uncontrollably, Alicia grabbed at Carolina, her eyes enlarged by fear and dripping tears. "You've got to help me."

Carolina, trying to grasp everything at once, to decipher the babble and make sense of the situation, hesitated.

"Agent Carolina, you've got to believe me. Look, I live with the White's down the hall. Tonight I was babysitting. I was like, bored, so I used Bud's binoculars and looked out the window. The killer knows I saw him. He'll come and shoot me too. You've got to believe me." Spittle running from the side of her mouth, snot ready to drip, Alicia sniffled and wiped her face with the back of her hand.

Carolina zeroed in on the one word that left her stunned. "Babysitting? There're kids left alone? How many?"

"Three babies. They're sleeping. I'll go and get them and bring them here. I just wasn't sure you'd be home, and I didn't want to scare them for nothing."

"Wait. When did this happen?"

"A few minutes ago, maybe five. I came here as soon as I remembered you were a cop. I'll get them."

"No, you'll stay right here and call 911. I'll go and check out the apartment. What number is it? Is the door locked?"

"No! Oh man, I forgot to lock the door or bring the keys. It's at the end of the hall on the left, Apartment 2020. The babies are alone with that killer." The teen slid her shaking hand through her long hair at the front, gathered it and threw it back over her shoulders.

"Calm down. Do as I told you. The phone's in the kitchen. Call the police and tell them what you told me. And whatever happens, don't leave this apartment. Only let me, or the guys with a badge come in. Got it?"

"Got it." Alicia ran for the kitchen, knocking over a chair on her way and ignoring it.

Rattled, using her training to control uncomfortable urges of running as far and fast as she could, Carolina reached behind her for her gun, turned the safety off and opened the door. She made sure it locked behind her and then checked the corridor, noticing the elevator light showing the last stop had been on their floor.

Which could mean nothing or...

Slowly, holding the gun in the two-handed aim taught at the academy, she made her way to the apartment down at the end of the hall. Ready to hurl, her stomach reacting violently to the sudden stress, she forcefully tamped down on the negative emotions. Reaching, she opened the door noiselessly and slipped inside.

Surveying the living room, she recognized the sweet odor one gets from a can of room spray. The view from the huge window caught her attention. *The girl could be telling the truth.* Suddenly, she heard a noise and quickly sought refuge behind the puffy couch sitting a few feet away from the wall.

A man, dressed in dark clothes and a mask, slipped out of the bedroom hallway and moved toward the kitchen. She saw him silhouetted in the soft lighting from under the counter and noticed instantly; he held a Glock with a silencer and looked completely comfortable while doing so.

Shit. The teen had called it right. He was here to clean up.

Unwilling to show herself, knowing that a killer wouldn't hesitate to shoot; she hoped he'd turn away from her to check the pantry. Then she could sneak up from behind and catch him unaware.

Before the plan could be implemented, distant sirens informed that the police had arrived. Now spooked, the killer headed for the exit.

Reluctant to let him escape, Carolina called out, her voice shrilly. "FBI. Hold it ri-right where you are. Drop your—"

Gunshots, aimed her way, thudding into the wall above her, stopped the rest of her speech. Dropping down again and peeking from the side of the sofa, she sent one bullet toward him but realized he'd already made a sprint for freedom. She heard the door crash open and running footsteps.

Quickly swallowing her reluctance to move, she followed to the staircase, reopening the closing door. She yanked her head back just in time as he sent a flurry of bullets her way. Not wanting to get shot, but needing to shadow the asshole, shaking badly, she glued her body to the wall and took her time.

Once she started moving, her feet slithered on the steps under her and she barely had enough time to grab at the railing. Savagely ripping the slippery, fuzzy socks from her feet, she dropped them on the ground and continued her chase.

On every floor, she peeked to see if she had a clear shot but had to hold her fire. The killer knew to keep to the wall, giving her less of an angle to take a chance. Floor after floor, she chased him down, praying no citizen looking for exercise would take the stairs.

Around the fourth floor, her anticipated nightmare came into play. A woman with her small dog opened the door, meaning to use the stairs. Seeing this happening, Carolina sent a volley of bullets at the killer to keep him from firing his own weapon and yelled at the same time, "Get back lady."

A scream from the woman and pitiful yaps from the leashed dog were heard before the door clanked shut. Thankful the woman wasn't near enough to become a hostage, Carolina continued her chase, gaining on him with every floor they hit.

Praying the police would automatically cover every exit, she hoped they'd be in place before the killer reached the bottom floor.

Obviously thinking the same way, the shooter didn't do the expected. He left the stairs on the second level and Carolina followed as soon as she reached that landing. Not sure what to expect, she carefully opened the stairway exit and checked the hall each way, right and left.

Nothing!

As if he'd vanished into thin air, there was no sign of him. Until she heard the scream and watched the door from the second apartment past the stairs get flung open, and a crazed woman emerged.

Thin as a rake, her hands flapping wildly, the

poor victim looked as if a complete breakdown was only seconds away. Sympathizing, knowing how she felt, Carolina rushed at her yelling, "Come this way."

"He sh-shot my husband." More screams erupted.

Carolina pulled her to the safety of the stairs, shook her to make her listen. "Ma'am, I need to know. Is the killer still in there?"

"No! He left. Over the balcony. He caught my husband opening the door and forced his way inside. He shot him and then went over the balcony. Oh, my God. I think he killed my man."

Chapter Five

Carolina took off like a shot, running into the apartment. First she headed for the poor bastard writhing in a pool of blood near the door. At a glance, she knew his superficial shoulder wound wouldn't end his life.

Ignoring the pungent coppery smell that threatened to bring her to her knees, she pulled a sweater off the back of a chair, bundled it and settled it over the injury. "The police are coming, sir. Hold onto this like a bandage and put pressure on it."

"That's m-my wife's favorite sweater. She'll be m-mad if I get blood on it."

"She'll get over it. You need it more than she does now."

"Oh? Did he shoot her?"

Did he sound wishful?

Sorry to dampen his optimistic contemplation, she answered, "No, she's in the corridor stairway, sir. She's upset, but fine."

"Oh, good." *Yep, now there was a distinct sound of sorrow. She'd have to share this one with her gramps. He'd love the irony.*

Back on the chase, she ran through the living room to the balcony to see if the assassin lay injured at the bottom after his crazy jump or if he'd made it safely and completely disappeared.

Within seconds, she knew he'd survived the leap and had left the scene. Being that they were on the side of the building, nowhere near the front where the police might have stopped him from escaping, she had no choice. Sighing, she leapt over the railing and prayed he wasn't waiting to put a bullet in her for her trouble.

Landing like a cat on the ground, perched low, she listened carefully. She heard groans and stumbling footsteps. It sounded as if he might have hurt himself when he landed. Figuring she'd have a chance to catch up with him, she gave chase.

In her mind, debating his choices, she decided he'd use the bushes for cover rather than stay in the open. Carolina followed. By the time she cleared the path and hit the front sidewalk, there wasn't another person nearby.

Most likely, he'd parked his vehicle closer to the opposite building where his first kill took place. He'd have made his way in that direction. Or at least, it's what she would have done. Damn, she should have thought of that instead of circling to the right.

"Stop right there. Drop your weapon and put your hands up where I can see them." The squeaky, shaky voice of a young cop came through loud and clear. She heard the fearful belligerence behind the order. Aware that nowadays cops shot first and asked questions later, especially untrained younger guys who didn't have the proper experience to deal with a perp holding a gun, she followed his instructions.

She dropped to her knees and laid the gun on the ground, then put both hands over her head where they would be seen. "I'm Special Agent Carolina Madison. Don't shoot."

Chapter Six

After the police were able to confirm that a hit had taken place in the exact apartment that Alicia had pointed out, they got serious.

While officers taped off certain areas in this living room where bullets had been fired, others began photographing the scene, bagging and tagging the evidence. The rest of them settled in the kitchen. Uniforms had been sent earlier to pick up the Whites and their friends, explain the circumstances and force them to return home.

It took hours for all the hullaballoo to settle down, the questions asked and answered.

Two couples who collected their babies left, but not before making a fuss, asking too many questions and getting close to ruining the crime scene. One of the inebriated women kept shooting photos with her phone and even tried taking a selfie with Alicia until the officer in charge put a stop to the nonsense.

All liquored up and still flying high, Carolina

could see Bud and Margo weren't taking the news of what had occurred well at all. Margo's face turned beet red when she found out that because Alicia had used binoculars she'd been forbidden to touch, she'd inadvertently witnessed a murder.

"Let me get this straight," Margo, her beer-soiled dress wrinkled and sliding off one shoulder, hovered over Alicia's chair. Her face mottled with fury, eyes bulging and bloodshot from booze, she ranted, "You used Bud's stuff without permission, saw some broad getting whacked and called the police before you called me? Is that what you're saying here?"

Alicia cowered in her chair, the blanket wrapped around her shoulders slipped, exposing her trembling. "I didn't know what to do, Margo. He saw me. I knew he'd come. I remembered you told me that Miss Madison was FBI, so I asked her to help."

"And you left the children. You weren't too worried about their safety, were you? Just about saving your own ass."

Carolina felt the urge to check out the bitch's neck size, which prompted her to put a stop to the twit's badgering. "Unless you've been in a similar situation, you have no idea what you'd do, Mrs. White. Alicia was smart. She asked me to help her and the babies, knowing it would take much longer for the police to get here."

Margo turned on her, vicious in her

condemnation. "And what the hell did you do? Shooting bullets in my place like some crazy TV cop, kids sleeping in the other room, I'm thinking to sue your ass. What would have happened if they'd woken up?"

"They didn't. I was there to make sure he didn't hurt anyone. Why do you think I went to the apartment rather than let Alicia return? Make no mistake, she wanted to. I made her stay at my place and call for help."

A small whiny voice broke into their heated altercation. "Licia. Me 'ant potty."

The young, sleepy-faced boy, his thin hair standing straight up, stood in the doorway, took one look at the mass of people in the room and ran straight for Alicia, his pudgy arms out to be picked up.

"Hi Buddy. Sure, Alicia'll take you to the bathroom, but then you need to go back to bed, honey, okay?" Alicia shrugged off her blanket and stumbled from the room, sheltering the clinging, droopy-diapered, heavy child.

The three cops stopped what they were doing to watch the youngster being carried from the room. Their silence spoke more than any words could say. Disgust filtered over the lead detective's face for a few seconds before he hid it behind professional courtesy.

Carolina, who'd caught his eye, acknowledged his slight nod, showing her agreement with his assessment. The Whites were scum.

From the moment Bud White had arrived home, he'd ranted over and over, "Where were you guys while killers were shooting innocent people? Huh? Nobody's safe in their own homes now. Crazy bastards! Running around with guns and breaking into apartments."

"Shut up, Bud. No one wants to hear your bullshit." Margo erupted, using her husband as her kicking post. "So, what are you going to do about our safety? He's out there, free as a bird, and he knows where Alicia lives."

Detective Crawly, the lead on the case – a solid man of mid-fifties with a full head of gray hair, a face decorated with pot marks and a keen intelligence – maintained a demeanor perfect for an officer of the law. "We'll have an officer stay here for the rest of the night, ma'am. I'll have my men escort you and your family to a hotel nearby while we finish our investigation. Don't worry, Mrs. White, we'll do everything we can to keep you safe."

"Oh yes you will, Detective. I'll see to that."

Showing a complete lack of empathy for the teen in her care, Margo White dropped her bombshell. She exploded at Alicia, who'd just returned to her place by the table. Before the teen could lift the blanket to replace it around her, Margo attacked. "And you, Miss Can't-keep-your-stupid-nose-to-yourself, you're outta here. Tonight! Pack up and get out. You hear me? We're not safe as long as he thinks you're still around."

Chapter Seven

Watching the youngster begging Margo to reconsider, Carolina felt her stomach juices swirl. Fervently wishing Margo would suffer, visions of her fat butt being kicked repeatedly began to form. Carolina hated small-minded, mean people, and she kept her hands away from her weapon in case she couldn't control sudden wild urges.

"Please, Margo. Don't do this. It wasn't my fault a killer broke into that lady's place."

"Who cares? You watched him kill her, and now you're too dangerous to be around. Bud and me'll have to move in with my folks for a while until he realizes you don't live here anymore. And my mom's a real pain in the ass, nutbar." She gestured rudely. "This is your stupid fault. Get out of my sight. Leave! Now! Let the cops take you back to the dump where we picked you up."

Alicia fled to her room. Unable to leave the poor

kid alone with her misery, Carolina made eye contact with a disgusted Detective Crawly and got a nod of permission. She followed the girl.

Disgust flooded. How anyone could call this tiny closet a room was beyond her. Seeing the rack of hooks for the girl's clothes and cloth linen baskets stacked against the wall rather than a dresser, Carolina took one of the black plastic bags a tearful Alicia had fetched and started to fill it.

Sneaking a peek at the teen had her guts roiling. Alicia needed sympathy and a feeling of security right now, not to be condemned and thrust out like she had no value. Carolina could hear her Gramps's voice in her head. He'd have been livid at the circumstances forced on this young girl.

Gathering as much as she could, Carolina bypassed a stained night table by the neatly-made twin-sized bed that held Alicia's precious items. She left them for Alicia to deal with.

An older model cell phone with a cracked screen was slipped into Alicia's newly donned jeans, and she carefully rolled her books and small personal items into a fuzzy purple cover that sat at the end of her bed.

Alicia trailed her hands over the plushness and her words offered insight to Carolina that told a story. "I won this blanket in a raffle at the mall. It's soft and pretty."

Sarcastic and not caring, Carolina said, "I'm surprised the white witch let you keep it."

Giggling at Carolina's pun, Alicia nodded. "She wanted me to give it to Buddy."

Shocked, Carolina replied, "To Mr. White?"

"No. The baby. Buddy Junior. But he gave it back to me. He's a pretty cool kid for only being two and a half years old. Acts like a spoiled brat when he's with his parents, but when we're alone, he's a sweetie."

"Seriously? He's a baby? That kid has to weigh over fifty pounds."

"They feed him junk food all the time, especially Bud. Buddy's the only one he shares his potato chips and cokes with."

Disgust obvious, Carolina changed the subject back to a safer topic and reached for the soft bundle before adding it to her bag. "I have a few of those cuddle-type throws around my place too. They come in handy on cold, rainy nights when watching TV."

"Yeah, well Margo took my TV. Who cares? It's tiny, the color kept fading and the picture was always blanking out."

Feeling her mounting anger ignite, Carolina wished she could use Margo for kick-boxing practice. Shrugging, keeping it cool, she did as her Poppa John told her to do as a kid. *Fix what you can and leave the rest to the karma Gods. In the end, they'll even things out.* Drawing in a large breath, she started a new line of questioning. "What did Margo mean about the dump?"

"Her and Bud took me in as a foster kid about a year ago, May fourteenth to be exact. She calls where I'd been living The Dump, but it's more like an institution where kids like me get shoved when no one wants them."

"Not to get personal but why did they foster you? It's obvious they have no affection for you."

"They needed a live-in free babysitter and housekeeper."

"Seriously?"

"Bud's okay sometimes, but creepy too, if you know what I mean." Alicia stared at Carolina, letting her eyes tell the story. Her meaning sent shivers spreading over Carolina. Incensed for the girl, she said nothing. But she'd sure as hell be looking into stopping the Whites from ever getting another girl from *The Dump*.

Not pussy-footing around anymore, Carolina asked point blank, "Did he ever force himself on you?"

"Not really. He started touching inappropriate places, but I warned him that Margo wouldn't like it, and I'd tell her if he didn't quit. So, he stopped. He lives under Margo's rules and only speaks up when she refuses him money for beer or forgets to buy his chips. Then the fight is on. Since she loves the stuff almost as much as he does, they don't fight very often."

"The place must cost a pretty penny. How do they make their living?"

"Margo works downtown as a bank accountant, and Bud is a divorce lawyer. His clients are all men, and he continuously complains about how *the bitches* take advantage of their poor husbands nowadays." Her finger gestures exaggerated the words as much as her voice.

"Alicia, how old are you? I saw your face when Margo mentioned *The Dump*. You don't intend to go back there, do you?"

"I'm fourteen, almost fifteen. The cops will drop me off, but if Jean Sowdon's still there, I'll leave. That cow knows exactly how to make life a living hell for those of us who... ahh, don't want her type of affection. She makes me sick. I can't go back to living like that again."

"Is she an employee?"

"No."

"Then I'll check into it, okay? You can't roam the streets right now, kid. That lunatic is out there. From what you've told me about the murder, it sounds like the work of a professional. One who gets paid to do his job cleanly and efficiently. He's not going to rest until he takes care of loose ends. For a man like that, finding you will be simple."

"And I'm a loose end."

"Yep."

"He saw me, maybe not my features because I'd turned the lights low, but he'd have seen enough to be able to identify me as the girl who lives here. Margo and Bud are both too fat for them to be mistaken as me."

"The question is, can you identify him? You refused to answer that when the detectives were questioning you, but I remember what you said earlier when you came to fetch me. You watched his *evil expression* were the words you used – and he knew it. Therefore, he wasn't wearing his mask like he was when he broke in here and I confronted him, right?"

Alicia's face paled, and she dropped onto the bed, black plastic deflating around her feet.

"Oh God, what am I going to do?"

Chapter Eight

Later that night at the unfamiliar police station, separated from the clingy teen, Carolina was grilled again for every tidbit of information she could share. Precise, with no unnecessary words, Carolina gave her statement.

Soon, Detective Crawly, along with his boss, Deputy Chief Eric Prowler, had her isolated in his office where Carolina felt ambushed. "Understand this, sir. The identity of the killer doesn't concern me. And don't think I haven't noticed that you're trying to coerce me into taking on an assignment." Carolina rubbed her hands on her jean-covered knees, glad she'd taken the time to change. "As interesting as this case is, my plans have been made. I've just finished a brutal undercover mission, and I'm heading out for a well-earned vacation."

Visions suddenly appeared reminding her of the

last few weeks. They were getting close to D-day and the many combined forces involved in the take-down of the gang she'd penetrated meant loose tongues could get them all killed. Understanding this, she'd lived on her nerves and bad dreams for too long, and the consequences were the rioting emotions she suddenly had to deal with when she faced danger or hard choices. Like earlier in the apartment, facing a killer – *my knees shook so bad, I almost lost it.*

Shuddering, stress signals began vibrating. She felt a tightening in her chest, the stifling feeling that she'd stop breathing if she didn't concentrate ramped up.

When everything had started to unravel those brutal days before the final showdown, these same disgusting emotions had first reared their ugly heads. She hated not being in control, weak, shaky and close to tears. Frailty had never concerned her in the past, and it sucked.

If she ever intended to get past this breakdown and back to doing her job efficiently, this shit had to be dealt with – doctor's orders. Time she considered her own health, he'd said. You desperately need some peace of mind. In fact, he'd warned her just that morning in no uncertain terms... no stress.

"Agent Madison, please don't misunderstand. Earlier, you revealed your competence in the way you handled the situation. We were impressed and very glad you were there."

Thing is – I was shitting myself every minute, metaphorically mind you.

"If there was anyone else we could turn to, it would be done. But these are the facts." The too-slender, pale-faced, frustrated man wiped his hand over his bushy, gray mustache for the third time in as many minutes. He looked over at the detective who'd so far kept his mouth shut.

A frown from the boss who'd begun to pace around the office got him talking. "The kid's smart, Carolina. Knows her rights and has a mind of her own. If we take her back to the previous institute, she'd be a sitting duck. Plus, her body language screamed she wouldn't be kosher with that proposal."

Remembering her earlier conversation with Alicia, Carolina grinned without humor and added, "You're right."

Again, smoothing his mustache, the pacing man came to a stop next to his detective and leaned back against his desk. "So, we promised to set her up with a female officer in a safe place. But... and get this straight... you're the only person she's willing to trust in that capacity."

What? "You're kidding me. She's a nice kid. I feel sorry for her, but right now, I'm not the protection she needs." Carolina shot to her feet, moved behind her chair and gripped the back, leaning her rebellious stomach hard against it.

Prowler lowered his voice to a level not so demanding, less confrontational. "I wouldn't even approach you if I hadn't cleared it with your boss, Carolina. He agrees with me that there's no time to waste. We need to move on this case."

"Why? Do you know the killer's identity?"

"We only know him as Dylan Ross. We've been told he's a black man with short-cropped hair, medium height and muscular. In the underworld, they call him Silverado because for his executions, he uses a silver .45 ACP – Automatic Colt Pistol – with pearl handles engraved with his nickname. Other than the silver bullets he likes to use, we haven't any DNA or photographs; the man is careful, and in each country he's used a different identity. In the last four years, he's been tagged for six major kills and is wanted by many governments, ours predominantly. As a gun for hire, he's considered one of the best and paid handsomely for his services. So whatever the victim did, someone willing to pay a lot of money wanted her dead and without any strings."

Detective Crawly added his two cents. "Look, this Ross character has been on our radar after three prime kills in the US... that we know of. Powerful people internationally, who've made a huge noise through their local Police and Interpol, demand action, too. If he's hunting in our territory, I'd sure like to be the cop to bring him down."

"And you figure he'll stick around to take care of

loose ends, meaning Alicia."

"Oh, yeah. He's not going anywhere until he cleans up this mess."

Zeroing in on something he said earlier, Carolina questioned, "You mentioned that you talked to my boss, Deputy Assistant Jake Crompton?"

"Yes. He hesitated to speak on your behalf, explained you'd just come off a grueling case, and he wouldn't be prone to forcing any new assignments on you right now. Said he'd leave it up to you, but would expect a report from you personally before you take on any role."

"In other words, he's agreeable but..." This didn't surprise Carolina. Her boss was a man who believed in respecting his people. He'd taken a shine to her from the first day he'd been assigned to the Bureau in his current capacity. The fact that he'd held back from making any serious personal overtures would be simply because Carolina had let him know right from the beginning... don't bother.

He'd asked her outright if his being a single dad had anything to do with her rejection, and she'd assured him that wasn't so. She was totally off any serious relationships, so his circumstances didn't matter.

She simply wasn't interested, not in him or any of the other men in the office who'd made advances... and the one woman, who'd only shrugged when Carolina's eagle eye had shut down her first attempt.

"Exactly, he's agreeable. Agent Madison, we'll refund all the costs of your vacation, anything you need, just as long as you can keep that kid alive so when we bring in that animal, she can identify him as the killer. He'll go down for the rest of his life. But without our only witness, Alicia Shoal, we have no case, only circumstantial evidence that any well-paid scumbag of a lawyer could oppose and get him his walking papers."

Heart-sore, Carolina stuck to her guns. "You don't understand, I'm burned out. I'm not giving up my vacation. I can't. The way I am now, I'm no good to anyone."

Bristling, Crawly added, "You were damn good earlier."

"Because my training kicked in. I had no time to think about what to do." Her pride wouldn't let her admit to the multitude of negative emotions she'd suffered.

Prowler approached. "What if you don't have to give up your vacation? What if we arrange everything so you just take the kid with you... into witness protection? We'll set you up in the same kind of accommodations you previously arranged, and you can choose wherever you want to go."

"I've already chosen my destination, Fort Lauderdale. There're reasons I decided on that city, family reasons that still stand."

Catching on to his boss's line of reasoning, Crawly added, "It could work, Carolina."

Prowler, still planning out loud, added, "We'd cover any costs, set up protection with the local authorities, whatever you need. All you have to do is enjoy a vacation with the poor kid who looks like no one's ever been kind to her. Help us catch this scumbag before he claims another kill, Agent Madison."

Carolina began laughing, her nerves unleashed. "Oh, you're good, Chief, smooth as stainless steel. Ever thought of the stage back when you were making up your mind what career to choose?"

Rubbing his mustache, a quick wink shared, he tried to keep a straight face and failed. "Did it work?"

"Let me talk to the kid, and we'll see. Okay?"

"Okay. But don't take too long. The sooner we get Alicia safely hidden, the better. In the meantime, we'll get a female detective to follow through on your flight as planned. She'll take up the residence you'd set up."

"That means you think he'll peg me as the female there tonight and come after me."

"Maybe. He's good. We don't want to take any chances. In case he ties you to Alicia, and decides you're another victim, I want a solid net put in place. Therefore, if you do play along with us, we need your itinerary, your tickets, everything."

Chapter Nine

In her spare bedroom, Carolina cleared away the jumble from her earlier packing and made room for Alicia and her plastic-bagged belongings.

"Can I really stay here with you?"

"Yeah, for now. With an officer on duty in the hallway by your old apartment and another guarding the entrance, it's a safe place. If the sleaze returns, you'll be protected. I have my weapon too in case he gets past security. We need to keep you alive so the department can make future arrangements."

Carolina thought back to earlier when she told the lead detective and his captain that she was on leave. *"I understand, Agent Madison, but you don't seem to get the gravity of our situation."*

Carolina slumped onto the bed; the pounding in her head hitting an all-time high.

Alicia's fingers snapped and brought Carolina

back. The kid's pale features screwed up, her shrewd expression surprising. "Something else happened. At the police station, after you talked to the Captain. I saw your face. They shared some information with you, didn't they?"

Carolina grinned. "You're too smart by a long shot, kiddo."

"Tell me about it? I get straight A's in most of my classes except for Math. And there I just play around because I can't stand the deranged teacher. She picks on some of the kids until she makes them cry. She's a noob, like Margo."

"A noob?"

"A nobody, a lowlife."

"Can't argue with you there."

"You didn't answer my question."

"I'd hoped you wouldn't notice."

"Like I said, I'm smart, when I'm not in my own way. And right now, I know something's going on. It's about me, and you're not sharing. Why did you really bring me here?"

Carolina heard the fear in the teen's voice. She surveyed Alicia's features and realized the girl was barely holding on. *Poor baby, she's been through so much. Right now, she needs sympathy... and a friend.*

"We called *The Dump* and Jean Sowdon's still registered."

"And...?"

"Blasted hell! You said you wouldn't stay if she was there. I couldn't very well, in all good conscience, let you roam the streets and get killed, now could I?"

"There're other institutions. Other places for kids like me. Why here?"

"Because!" Carolina swiped at the golden-red curls bunched near her ears and blew at the mass on her forehead. "Man, your tough." She paced the room, her sexy pajama bottoms replaced earlier by a pair of form-fitting jeans that hugged her figure and had pockets where she slid her hands to stop their shaking. *Fucking stress!* "Look, we know who the killer is now, and he's not a man to be ignored."

"You know? How?"

"You told us by your description."

"No I didn't. All I said was he was a short-haired, black man with a fancy, silver gun."

"Yes."

"Yes, what? Oh..."

"Right. The silver gun gave him away. His name is Dylan Ross, known by officials as Silverado. Among other weapons, he most often uses a silver pistol when he's on the job as the executioner. In the last four years, he's been wanted by quite a few governments, ours predominantly. The man is freaky smart, a gun for hire and employs himself without prejudice by those willing to pay top dollar."

"Without prejudice?"

"He wouldn't care if it's a man, a woman or a nosy teenager."

Nodding, Alicia taunted, "If they know so much about him, why haven't they caught him?"

"Like I said, he's freaky smart. Look, we actually know very little, other than one of his names, and now what you've told us. He's brilliant at camouflaging himself. Using makeup, he's passed as both white and black and has umpteen identities. His MO includes breaking in, doing his job without there being any witnesses, and disappearing. Because of that, we've never been able to make an arrest. Other than the silver casings from the bullets he likes to use, we have nothing."

"I'm the only witness."

"Yes. You said you'd never forget what he looked like. That you saw enough to identify him."

"I did tell you that, but maybe I lied."

Carolina moved to stand in front of Alicia and saw the fear she couldn't hide. The damn kid was petrified.

"Were you? Lying?"

Alicia slumped, her shoulders curled toward her chest, her appearance suddenly taking on the look of a tired old lady. "He's nasty – a killer with a rep for staying under the radar and getting his prey?"

"'Fraid so."

"Which means – I'm screwed."

"Not if you let the government take you into the witness protection program. They explained tonight that they're willing to send you away and keep you safe until he's caught and on trial."

"Explained! Like they never let up. Talk about pressure. I felt like I was sitting on a burner and they kept turning the heat higher."

Needing to explain, Carolina added, "The authorities want this guy – bad."

"And I want you. In my heart, I know I'll only be safe with you. Is that so wrong? Am I being greedy?"

"No."

"But it's a problem." Alicia gauged Carolina's face, her dark eyes questioning.

"Yes."

"Then the first chance I get, I'll disappear."

Chapter Ten

"Why are you leaving me here? I want to go with you." Alicia's whine scored a direct hit.

"Sorry, kid. I can't take you this time. It's personal business. I'll only be gone for a couple hours, I promise. Just a loose end I need to tie up."

"I'm scared without you nearby, Carolina; terrified, actually. I'll be sick the whole time you're gone. Please, can't I come with you?"

From the moment Carolina promised to keep Alicia safe, to be her guardian in witness protection, the girl had become weirdly attached.

Carolina forced her voice to stay calm rather than losing her cookies at Alicia. Frustrated already about the phone call to Prowler – the one where she'd agreed to take on the safety of their witness – she now faced explaining the change in plans to her grandfather.

"Kid, back off."

Before the last syllable had left Carolina's raised voice, Alicia's demeanor changed from beseeching to totally distressed.

Calm down, bitch... it's not her fault.

"God, I'm sorry, Alicia." Carolina sucked in some air and lowered her voice. "Kiddo, you can't be seen with me. You know we're leaving later today, right. And we'll be together until the trial. But you need to give me these couple of hours. I made plans that I need to complete in case anyone is watching."

"I'm sorry. Detective Crawly explained it all to me."

"See, that's right. In the meantime, one of their stipulations is for me to carry on as if nothing has changed. While I'm away, Officer Dale, Melissa, the cop who'll be taking my previously planned trip, will be here to switch her things into my suitcases, etc. You'll have company while I'm gone. Okay?"

"He said she'd be bringing a file with our new identities that we have to memorize."

"Yes. Studying it will help pass the time. From now on you need to remember to call me Charli."

"Why Charli?"

"It's a nickname my Gramps gave me when I was younger. I'm used to it. Kiddo, I gotta go."

"You'll be safe?"

Ahh... her inner lightbulb ignited. *The kid isn't scared for herself, she's worried for me.* Carolina's attitude melted, and she softened her tone. "Yes, honey. Give me an hour, two tops."

Alicia swallowed, her eyes filling. She blinked rapidly and held out her hand. "I'm sorry. I'm not usually such a baby. I don't want to be a burden."

If she was a hard-hearted woman, Carolina might have taken her hand briefly and made light of the situation. But as much as she'd buried her young-girl tendencies as a loving, huggy person, this was one time she couldn't block herself.

She put her arms around Alicia and smoothed her long hair while the youngster clung tightly, a suspicious sob low but clear. "Hey baby, we're gonna be glued at the hip from now on. And no need to be scared when you're with me. I'm FBI and I don't take any prisoners, right. That asshole comes anywhere near us, and I'll plug that varmint right between his beady little black eyes. Deal?"

Laughing shakily, Alicia nodded and leaned back. "Deal. But just so you know, his eyes were anything but beady."

"Yeah? Well, when we get to Florida, they'll have a sketch artist working with you so you can bring him to life for all of us."

"And photos from the criminal website too?"

"Yes."

The doorbell rang to break up their embrace, but before Carolina could drop her arms, Alicia gave another tight squeeze and whispered, "No one's ever hugged me like this before. Thank you."

"Oh baby, you are *so* welcome." Carolina caressed her cheek before heading to the hallway to let in her decoy. With the back of her hand, she swiped at her own cheek before opening the door.

Poor, kid...

***

In the same booth that Charli and her grandfather often frequented at his favorite diner, Charli finished her thick vanilla milkshake and ate the last bite of her heavenly scented Polish dog. When her food had arrived, the smells of her most passionate teenage junk food assaulted and her hunger had taken over.

She'd worried over this meeting, knew it had to happen and that the police escort would make arrangements so they couldn't be followed. Surrounded by protection from others in her department, they'd driven her to this meeting. At the same time, her boss, Jake Crompton, a man who her grandfather would recognize, had fetched John Madison personally from his lodge, telling him that Charli would meet him at the diner.

When the two men had walked in, Charli had seen her boss's expression, and it spoke volumes. *You can't tell the old man anything, Carolina.* They'd discussed some of the details of the case earlier that morning, and he'd urged her to reconsider putting herself in another stress situation. He'd read the FBI psychologist's report and knew that she'd suffered through more than they would ever ask of her. But when she explained about Alicia Shoal and her fears, he'd understood why she had even considered the assignment.

Jake asked to speak to her alone for a few minutes and after she'd hugged the old man and got him settled in his place, she walked with her boss to the back of the big room and into a hallway leading to the restrooms.

"Thanks so much for bringing Grandfather here for me. I couldn't leave him without any explanations and saying a proper good-bye. He'd never forgive me."

"You're wrong, Carolina. That old guy adores you, thinks you walk on water. I'm just sorry about his vacation in Fort Lauderdale. He told me about all your plans for when he was to join you. Let's hope this assignment is over quickly, and you can still have him visit."

Charli stared at the good-looker, her expression as serious as steel. "My vacation time will be banked for when this is over, that's what they led me to believe."

Jake lifted his hand to pat her arm, and she forced herself not to flinch. "We'll take care of it, Carolina. You'll get your time off. I stopped by your place for a few minutes just after you'd left and met the kid. I see why you feel there's no choice. She's dependent on you; refused to even consider another agent."

"She's terrified."

"Don't blame her. It couldn't have been easy watching someone get killed."

A quick vision of herself standing over the body of the drug runner she'd just shot appeared in her head, and she shoved it back into purgatory where she'd forced it weeks ago. "It isn't."

Jake's sympathized searching of her features and his quick nod let her know he understood. "Madison, I don't want to lose one of my best Drug Enforcement Agents over this. You be careful, and make use of the protection from the local guys wherever you end up."

"You don't know?"

"The SPD refused to leak any information about which city or even state they planned on sending you. Just take every reasonable precaution. And call me as soon as you're free. In the meantime, the department will be pulling out all the stops to find Dylan Ross. We'll get him sooner or later, don't doubt it."

"Let's hope its sooner."

He laughed and took her hand. "Take care." He glanced up over her shoulder and grinned welcomingly. "Chief Prowler."

"Good to see you, Jake."

"I was just leaving. You take good care of this agent; she's an asset to the Bureau in every way."

"You have my word."

Carolina watched Jake stride over to first shake hands with her grandfather, and then to the door where a black SUV and driver waited.

Prowler watched with her and once the

Assistant to the Deputy had departed, he got her attention. "I've arranged with a friend of my brother's, Blake Sebastian, a Major with the FLPD to take you on as a special favor to me. He's a brave cop, has risen through the ranks quickly and will be your partner in keeping Alicia safe."

Charli had been briefed by Crawly. "I have no problem with that part, but why did you have to build in a romantic relationship?"

"All work and no play." He saw her expression and laughed.

"Kidding. He needs to get close, fast. This seemed to be a way to cut through the preliminaries of the first meet. You'll have to let him in, Carolina. He's taken on this assignment himself as a favor, so play nice."

Teasing now, she added, "Play – like in playing around? Trust me, that ain't going to happen."

Smug, his grin speaking volumes, "You haven't met the man yet. Good luck, Agent."

She watched him stride to the entrance, and then she took her seat. It felt wonderful to relax with her beloved companion and enjoy food she only allowed herself to eat when they visited this joint once a month.

It didn't take long before she found herself on the defense. "Popsicle, you can't ride me like this." Charli used her childhood nickname to soften her old grandfather so he would relent on his woe-is-me attitude. "You know I can't divulge certain aspects of my job. All I can say is this: I'll be working on a highly sensitive case, and I don't know when I'll be able to contact you. It's just that simple."

"Oh sure, simple for you. Here I am dying—"

"What?" She rushed to share his side of the booth, her hand reaching for his. "Did the doctors find something wrong?" Charli's heart dropped to the floor and lay there writhing.

"Oh, for heaven's sake, kid. I meant that literally. I'm ninety-years-old, brat. I can't live forever. I wanted this trip to Fort Lauderdale as a kind of au revoir, to leave you with memories, to be my swan song, to be a fun time with my little girl, to—"

"Okay! Enough already! The guilt is so heavy, I'll be on my knees begging for forgiveness with one more 'to be'." She giggled at her gramps' cheeky grin, his obvious enjoyment of her teasing. It was this way between them every time they were together. Truth is, she loved spending time with her old gramps and having to stop their original plans was killing her.

But taking on witness protection meant cutting ties with everyone in her circle until they captured the killer. Seeing as Gramps was the main person for her, the only one who meant anything in her life, protecting him meant discontinuing all communication for the immediate future.

And cutting off her arm might be less painful, especially when John Madison didn't intend to be left out. The wily old bugger could be as sniveling as any teenager begging to go to *the party* of the year where all the popular kids would be hanging out.

He didn't take no easily, didn't like having his plans messed with and wasn't willing to be agreeable.

"There's got to be a way we can be in communication. What about those burner phones you see them using on all the cop shows. We can get a couple of those so I can talk to you."

"It's against the rules, Gramps." The guilt doubled when she saw the regret in his eyes, and knew he'd started to sense the danger. "You know I wouldn't have taken on this assignment lightly. Trust me, okay? I'll be safe; it'll be like I'm taking a vacation, only I won't be alone. And if there's any way I can contact you, I will."

He put his gnarled, working-man's hands on both sides of her face to lift her eyes his way. "I can't lose you, girl."

"Just for a short while, Gramps. But I'll be back, and then we'll take that vacation you've been looking forward to so much."

"You're sure I can't tag along this time?"

"No way. You're too precious to take any risks with."

"Risks?"

Fu-ck!

Chapter Eleven

Charli and Kayla followed the security cop dressed like a pilot through a long hallway and into the regular terminal. The hectic Fort Lauderdale airport pulsed with a multitude of busy people from all walks of life.

"From now on kid, we can't screw up. I'm Charli Steele, and you're my fifteen-year-old stepsister, Kayla Steele. Got it?" They'd been practicing while on the plane, but Alicia didn't take to role-playing easily and kept slipping. "Our lives could depend on us paying attention to details, right?"

"Right. I'll be careful, I promise."

"Good. Let the show begin."

She felt Kayla take her hand, and she gave the girl's fingers a squeeze.

On her guard, Special Agent Carolina, now an ordinary book editor on vacation, Charli Steele, looked for anything out of place. She picked out the two cops on surveillance without any trouble.

Trained to make those calls, she ignored both the short-haired, muscle-type nonchalantly reading the paper, and the pretty red-headed woman at the coffee dispenser with the bulge under her jacket.

According to Chief Prowler, they were to be met by an old friend of his brother's, a Blake Sebastian, Major with the Fort Lauderdale police. He would deliver them to their new residence and set up his parameters for the witness protection their local office would be providing.

Having the FLPD assistance in the case made Charli breathe a hell of a lot easier. What she didn't quite like was the fact that they'd made up a pseudo-engagement that had lasted a short time between her and Blake while they'd been in college. He would be meeting them as an old flame, her and her younger sister.

She scanned the airport lounge for a tall man, an intimidating police Major. From the photo they'd added to her package, he'd looked lean with reddish-blonde hair, longish and styled, and glowing green eyes that must get him a lot of dates.

Since they'd made a side note about his single status and abundance of girlfriends, she didn't know if it was meant as a warning to keep him at arm's length or as an incentive for her to be glad she'd taken the case.

Lost in her thoughts, Charli didn't see the man

approaching on her right. Suddenly, arms wrapped around her and lifted her in the air. Green stunners, skimming her face and her recently-dyed blonde hair, brightened with interest. "Charli, sweetheart, how are you?"

Quick as a wink, Charli readied herself to retaliate and remembering the scenario just in time, she stopped. Rather than karate chop his neck, she used her raised hand to slap at his shoulder in a seemingly playful way. "Hey, Romeo, how's life?"

Lowering her stiff body, Blake rotated his arm as if to shake off pain. "Life is phenomenal now that you're back in it. You look good, honey, real good." Was he playing with her on purpose? Who knew for sure? But his profuse boldness pushed a lot of her buttons. And when his eyes toured her body like she was a flea-market bargain, she just wanted to slap him again... harder.

Instead, she shared a tight smile, playing her role. "You, too, Sweetykins. Put on a little weight since I saw you last? I almost didn't recognize you."

He grinned, his too-handsome-to-live-outside-of-Hollywood smile flashed. When he lifted his hand, he enjoyed her determination not to flinch and pull away. Instead, he laughed when the light in her marble-gray eyes flashed a warning. "I see by these ringlets, you got yourself one of those perm things. I always loved your hair without all these... ahh coils." He let go of the curl he'd pulled and watched it rewind to nestle on her shoulder.

Since her *coils* were natural, she twisted her head to the side, the warning obvious. "Don't you remember my hair straightener? And the times I'd keep you waiting?"

"Sure, now that you mention it. Just so you know, you were always worth those extra hours, baby."

Hours?

Bastard!

Kayla moved in closer to support Charli and caught Blake's attention. Charli held her breath, waiting to see if he would step out of line with her charge.

He said nothing, just held out his hand.

Kayla took it and said, "I'm Charli's stepsister, Kayla." Nerves in the teen's voice were apparent to Charli, but she had no doubt they would skim over Romeo's thick head of hair.

"I know. Charli sent me your picture. But it didn't do you justice, Kayla. You're even prettier than I expected." His smooth male voice, husky with admiration, must be a real turn-on to the ladies he supposedly has lined up.

"Thank you," Kayla simpered.

Charli just rolled her eyes and shared her sneer when her reaction caught his attention. It brought an even bigger grin, and she sensed he was enjoying her response.

"Blak-ie, were you coming to meet my plane,

baby?" A playboy bunny look-alike sidled up to Blake, wrapped her arms around his middle and hugged. Then she arched her head so she could kiss his mouth, a kiss he certainly didn't try to dodge. On the contrary, he engaged in the by-play with obvious enjoyment, his hand lowering to her backside and squeezing.

That action lifted her mini skirt above the decency level and Charli watched men walk into others, trip over their bags and get glares from their women when the plump bottom was revealed for their pleasure.

Oh, for God's sake! Not impressed whatsoever, Charli decided enough was enough. She turned her glare away from the sight in time to see the red-headed undercover cop shrug with resignation. Charli could have sworn the girl looked wishful, even envious before she got back on the job of watching for any disturbances.

Her glance swung to the other cop; he definitely looked envious. *What the hell?*

Enough...

Charli dug her fingers into Blake's arm to get his attention. "Sugar-bunny. Kayla and I will grab our bags and wait for you in the baggage area." Simpering at his gorgeous friend, Charli wriggled her fingers before heading in the opposite direction. "Bye now."

Kayla followed her, but like so many others, her eyes stayed glued to the action. "She's gorgeous."

"Tanned blondes with inflatable butts and boobs do not always equate to good people. For example, she didn't even notice that *Blak-ie* had company. Nor did she introduce herself in the classy way you did. Sorry, kiddo. She gets an F in my book."

Kayla giggled knowingly. "Does that stand for failing?"

Since it really stood for fuck-up, Charli had to think fast. "Nah. More like forget it. Not worth the time or trouble."

"I'd use the F with an O, like in eff off, but if I swear, you'll give *me* that look."

Charli had no trouble translating eff off, but she had to ask, "What look?"

"The *don't*... like in *don't you do it* look. It's quite impressive. Never knew anyone else whose eyes could speak volumes while her mouth said nothing."

Laughing out loud, totally enjoying the exchange, Charli didn't see Blake sidle up to join them once again.

"You look pretty when you laugh, Charli. Anyone ever tell you that before? You should do it more often."

Her good mood fading, sourness creeping back in, Charli retorted. "You ready to take us home now? Or do you have a date?"

Before he could answer, three women walked past, heading to the bar/restaurant just behind where they stood. Two of them expressed greetings and gestured to Blake, wiggling their fingers flirtatiously and smiling, invitations plain.

"Sorry, ladies. I'm here to pick up an old college friend. Next time." He waved them away and had the audacity to wink at Kayla and make an off-side remark to Charli. "I'm well-known in the city."

"You mean you have a reputation. That's a whole different topic, *Blak-ie*." Charli gathered her suitcase, nodded at Kayla to do the same and headed in the direction of the nearest exit. "Let's get out of here before the poor man gets accosted again."

***

On their drive to wherever Blake had set them up, Charli, who'd opted for the back seat, fumed while Kayla and Blake shared stories and enjoyed each other's company.

What an ass! He obviously thought he was God's gift to the Fort Lauderdale ladies, and he didn't hide the fact that he loved their attention. How were they supposed to play the part of a reuniting couple, falling back in love? It was ridiculous. She couldn't stand the man.

Admittedly, he looked better than most officers in uniform but she put that down to his height. Tall for a woman, he'd topped her by a good six or seven inches. But just because his well-formed lean body and muscular arms picked her up as if she weighed less than a child, she wouldn't let admiration seep into her overall impression of the guy. He was a conceited ass, pure and simple.

Any man who so obviously adored being adored had failings, immense failings. And Charli had no time for that nonsense. Pain began to build in her neck, and she reached for her purse to get her pill bottle. If she didn't stay on top of these migraines, she'd be no good to anyone.

After she dry-swallowed the coated Tylenol, she caught his sharp-eyed stare in the rearview mirror, his eyebrow lifted questioningly.

Without thinking, she responded, "Birth control."

He smirked.

She choked.

Bloody hell!

Chapter Twelve

When Blake pulled into a driveway on Lauderdale Beach belonging to a stunning property with an overall white, Greek Island appearance, Charli's pulse began to race. This reminded her of the house she'd rented a few weeks ago.

When they parked the car in the circular driveway and stepped out, the fragrance from the nearby beach intermingled with the multitude of lush flowering bushes. *Now this is more like it!* Her chest muscles relaxed and her tight nerves lightened considerably.

Heavenly!

Kayla gushed her enthusiasm. "Wow! This place is goat."

Both Blake and Charli stopped and stared at her until she flushed and added, "Greatest of all time!"

Charli answered, "Of course that's what it means." She made a face and Kayla laughed.

Blake joined in. "Kids have their own language today. At the precinct, we need a dictionary to be able to hold a conversation." He waved at the house. "Come on, I'll show you around."

The sprawling house appeared larger from the outside, but the open floor plan inside captured the true South Florida look she'd fallen in love with when searching for her own choice of a rental.

Not that she'd ever expect to live in such luxury as a permanent home, the thought of vacationing in this beachside dream bungalow produced a real smile. It started on her lips and unwound the tightness, the burden, the heavy weight she'd felt since taking on this job.

Until she saw the man's shoes in the hallway and the books scattered around the living room. It looked as if someone lived here. She glanced over at the kitchen and saw the coffee pot half empty, sitting on the island, and the mug still showing dregs of the dark beverage.

Hold it! They'd promised her a rental; at least they'd conveyed that impression during her last discussion with Detective Crawly and Deputy Chief Prowler. A house for Kayla and her to share – only them.

She stood in one spot and continued to spy each area and the mounting evidence affirmed her suspicions, someone occupied this house. "Who lives here?" She gritted the words through her teeth, holding back on the cuss ones she really wanted to shout.

Blake stopped carrying Kayla's suitcases and let them down slowly. "It's my house. We decided it would be best for you to have the extra protection this place has installed." He pointed to the security pad near the entrance, bragging, "A buddy installed this gadget and it's the newest of the new." He then slid back a large wall section to show off a screen with four security monitors giving a view of each side of the house. "A few break-ins on the street last year prompted me to get the house protected. And get this," he picked up a small R2D2 looking camera, "I can also check an app on my phone anytime to see what's happening in most areas inside the house. We set up these individual room cameras..."

Charli's shocked glare stopped his bragging.

"Which, I'll take down while you girls are here."

"Yes, you will." Charli's rigid tone brooked no argument. Turning to him, her hands on her hips, and her rising temper *almost* under control, she asked pleasantly, "And where do you intend to live while we take over *your* house?"

Pretending to misunderstand the signals, he winked at Kayla and answered mischievously, "Well sweetykins, I intended to stay in my bedroom during the night. During the day, while I'm at work, I'll leave you two ladies to your own devices. That's the deal I made with Prowler, and he led me to believe you were in agreement."

Charli erupted, "Over my dead body, Bub. Those two fools knew my plans for some down time and that means being alone." Kayla's jerking movement caught Charli's attention and stopped her tirade. She forced herself to calm down and added, "I meant being alone with Kayla. Not entertaining a womanizing playboy every night."

Blake blinked; his grin slow to appear. "Darlin', you won't have to entertain me. I can find that kind of distraction any time I want." His sincere tone let her know he didn't boast. He just stated a fact.

Ooohh! The man rubbed her the wrong way.

"Good to know. It still isn't part of the deal. Come on, Kayla. We'll find a place of our own."

She picked up the suitcase she'd refused to let him carry and started for the front door.

"Where will you go, Agent Madison?" His official tone stopped her.

"Away from here... and you."

"But Charli, we can't leave. This is where the cops want us to stay," Kayla's pleading tone stopped her hand in midair – two inches from the doorknob.

Son of a bitch! She turned and glared in Blake's direction. "The only, and I mean *only* way I'll stay is if you leave us the house and go to a hotel. I'm talking a luxury place; and I'll pay all your expenses."

"I can do that."

Taking a deep breath of relief, she stuttered, "Y-you can?" Her nerves stopped short-circuiting, skidded to a crawl and settled back into a somewhat normal rhythm.

"For a few days, to let you gals get your bearings. But I'll be in and out, so expect it."

"Call first."

"I can do that too."

"Okay then. Okay." She watched Kayla doing a little wiggly, in-place-dance and realized for the first time that the house had hooked the kid as much as it had pleased her.

"Tomorrow is soon enough to get you girls on par with what we set in place – the school, your job, everything you'll need. In the meantime, there's good security on the property and motion lights set up outside. Come with me, I'll show you around. "

Charli had to admit that for a bachelor, the man kept a nice house. And the well-outfitted gym and spacious pool out back drew both her and Kayla. Letting down her guard, she pivoted, almost slamming into the man. His hands caught her but let go instantly, as if he'd been scalded, his features comically reacting.

"It's a beautiful home." Truth rang in her voice, and she had no idea why she felt the need to give him the compliment. Maybe because he'd been sympathetic about her need for privacy. Or maybe because he knew women, and he played her. It didn't matter, she could breathe again.

Chapter Thirteen

Driving back to the office, Blake pondered his situation. He had no idea why he'd agreed to Charli's ridiculous ultimatum. After all, they were two law officers forced together in a sticky situation of needing to protect Kayla.

If Silverado made it his business to find the girl, the fucker would do it by following the trail they hadn't taken enough time to bury properly. With the dude's contacts throughout the dark web and obvious expertise online, Blake had no doubt they could be in danger sooner rather than later.

After Chief Prowler had called him, explaining the situation and asked for his assistance, he'd made it his business to call his buddy, top media expert, whiz hacker and all-around computer genius, Tod Rawlins.

Tod wasn't on the force, though Blake often called on him. With Blake's assistance, he'd barely kept his ass out of the slammer – the kid skimmed close to the line more often than not. To pay back the favor, he'd take on special jobs for Blake when they needed someone with his special skills.

At his tender age of nineteen, he managed his own computer business building squeaky-clean websites for people who required privacy and were willing to pay big bucks to ensure they had the best.

Once Blake had explained the reasons why he needed his help, Tod became involved, dug deep and the stuff he found scared the shit out of them both. They'd pieced together a lot of material and one thing became very clear. This killer had no conscience.

Reading over Tod's numerous notes had enlightened him to the fact that the prick, Ross, loved to kill, plain and simple. And he did it well. Anyone who left his calling card at each scene – his ritual for bragging to law enforcement – that person was one sick dude.

It didn't matter the gender or age of his victims. Personally, Blake wondered if the FBI had uncovered *all* the murders Silverado actually committed. If not, the one's where he'd followed his MO and left the silver bullet casing as his calling card were sufficient to give them an insight into the sociopathic sicko.

His narcissistic tendencies, that craved attention, might be his greatest downfall.

Obviously, he loved his chosen line of work, which paid him big money. And... his reputation mattered; certainly enough where he'd need to cauterize loose ends, like a witness who could place him as the killer.

Blake stopped at a red light, and a beautiful woman crossed in front of his assigned SUV. The way she sauntered – the swaggering carriage of her fine body – brought another to mind, Special Agent Charli Madison.

Hold it bud, get it right. Her name used to be that. Now she'll be known as plain old Charli Steele.

Which would be an oxymoron of huge proportions; that chick was anything but old or plain.

Her image appeared from memory, and his hands tightened on the steering wheel. She had a way about her that drew him in and repelled him all at the same time.

He envisioned capturing the gaze from her melting brown eyes while he scattered light kisses over the high cheek bones that gave her a model-like appearance. Then he'd shift his attention and place scalding, searching kisses on her lush lips, drain her resistance. He wouldn't stop until she sighed his name with delight.

Shifting his butt, he turned up the air conditioner.

Earlier, he'd teased her about her curls, but when he'd touched the silkiness, his hands had itched to dig in and clutch the mass, to draw her closer so he could teach her a lesson.

Then she'd spoke, and the craving had faded. He'd wished to be anywhere but in the same space as her all-seeing eyes and smirking, knowledgeable stare that saw deep inside him, into places no one got to inspect... not even himself.

Waiting for the light to change, he again questioned his reluctance to push Charli on their accommodations. He'd sensed her dislike and it intrigued him. Not one to brag or take smug, self-satisfied selfies, nonetheless, women liked him. All of them. He hadn't met one yet who didn't. Correction – he'd just met her.

And as much as he'd have enjoyed continuing to stick pins in her prickly attitude, to get her to retaliate, the look of horror on Kayla's face had prompted his surrender.

For some strange reason he didn't want to investigate too closely, he'd taken to the kid. And she'd gotten all dreamy-eyed about staying at his house. She'd been thrilled, and something had told him that Kayla didn't often get her wishes granted.

Only a cad would have burst her bubble and let Charli follow through on her challenge to leave. He couldn't do it. He liked looking at himself in the mirror every day without recriminations.

A screech, followed by a tell-tale thud, caught his attention, drawing his mind away from the introspection he'd been caught up in. He turned in the direction of the noise in time to see an older-model red Ford Focus back away from the pedestrian lying on the pavement and shoot up Las Olas Boulevard, swerving in and out of lanes, a heavy foot on the gas pedal.

Blake veered to a stop, and saw a nearby officer on foot, heading to the victim. He threw his vehicle back in gear and took off after the perpetrator of the hit and run.

Pushing the button on his steering wheel, he voice-activated the car phone to get headquarters. Calling in the crime, he asked for back-up and gave the particulars of the vehicle he was pursuing, his location, and the license plate number he'd read when he'd gotten close enough to see the plates.

Then he backed off, rather than push the wild driver into doing something they'd regret... like hitting someone else. *Fuck!* Too late. The erratic driver plowed into a vehicle just pulling out of a parking spot and creamed the driver's side badly. Before the maniac could pull back into traffic, Blake exited his SUV and ran up to the driver's side. His badge in front, he'd palmed his gun, just in case.

Once close enough to the driver, his warning rang out, "FLPD, let me see your hands. Get them both on the steering wheel. Do it now, man!"

The inebriated driver peered up, his eyes wild, dirty-blonde hair standing out around his scruffy, flushed face. He ignored the demands and tried to open the door. Stuttering explanations, his voice whiny and cajoling, he played the fool card like so many stupid offenders do, thinking the cops would stand down.

"It's okay, *ocifer*. I'm on business and in a hurry. Give me my fine, and I'll b-be on my way."

Blake held the gun out front now; making sure it was in full sight of the idiot so he'd follow orders. "No fines, the charge is hit and run, sir. We'll be taking a little trip downtown." Blake's slight adrenalin rush gave him a high he'd missed. God, it was good to be back on the streets, making an arrest, protecting the innocent.

While absorbed, self-satisfaction working its influence, the skinny driver saw his chance. He slammed his door open hard, smashing it into Blake. Caught off guard, Blake flew back and barely managed to retain possession of his gun. Once he got his bearings, he saw the driver running, hell bent for freedom, hightailing it up the street to disappear inside a local bar and restaurant.

Shit!

He spoke to the injured person, who'd left her car to stumble over and sit on the curb, blood running in a thin line from her forehead. "Are you okay Ma'am? Can you call an ambulance?"

"I'm fine, officer. Just go and get that son of a bitch before he kills someone."

He heard the sirens just then and within a few seconds, two cop cars pulled up to the scene.

Leaving her in good hands, Blake took off after the assailant.

At full speed, he headed inside to see a table upturned and one of the waiters on his ass in a mess. Another employee, shocked and scared looked on.

"Which way did the guy go?" Blake's tone cut through their distress and the one on the floor pointed to a hallway leading to the kitchen. "Out the back."

Blake ran there in time to see the culprit cut through to the next street and dodge the first lane of traffic. Running to catch up, Blake cleared the parked car in front of him, his ass sliding across the hood like a stunt man in a movie.

A thud, sounding the same as the earlier commotion, told him what had happened. Sure enough, the Karma God's were smiling. The idiot on the pavement, cussing, howling, clutching his leg, was the perpetrator of the first hit and run.

Satisfaction settled in as Blake approached the accident and calmed the female driver who'd correctly exited her vehicle and was approaching the victim. "I swear officer, I didn't see him. He came out of nowhere."

Blake smiled and patted her arm, "I'm your witness, ma'am. You didn't have a chance. He ran right in front of your car, didn't he?"

"Fuck you, man. I only did that because you were chasing me." The whiner spit out his vitriol, madder 'n hell at being caught. He tried to stand and fell backwards, then swore again.

Blake smiled and held out his badge. "Sir, I showed this to you at your window. I gave you instructions, and you not only ignored them, you left the scene of yet another accident. So guess what? It's my pleasure to inform you, you're under arrest. And when I get through writing my report, you'll be sporting white hair and a walker by the time the judge consents to give you back your license."

The gathering crowd began to clap, and it brought Blake's attention to the many cellphones pointed in his direction.

His famous grin at the photo-takers appeared at dinnertime on the nightly news.

Chapter Fourteen

That evening, after an afternoon spent lazing by the gorgeous white-walled, enclosed yard that housed the kidney-shaped pool and reminded Kayla of photos of a Greek Island hotel, Kayla and Charli scrounged for food in the kitchen.

Earlier, Charli had slept in the shade of the royal blue umbrella, catching up on a well-earned rest, while Kayla played on her new burner phone. With implicit instructions not to search for her old friends or contact them in any way, she resisted temptation.

How she'd have loved to send selfies with the pool in the background, an unmistakable finger to those bitches who thrived on meanness. Instead, she'd watched her new protector rest easy. Even if she was young, anyone who cared could see that Charli needed to relax.

Kayla would stay quiet and give her space so she

could rejuvenate and not be sorry for taking on her safety. In her book, Charli was aces. Alicia, Kayla, whoever they wanted her to be, needed her.

Chuckling to herself about the instructions that she contact no one in her past, she pushed away the sad. Like she cared about anyone enough to bother? She had no problem following those instructions. Not only did her safety depend on her behaving, but Charli had put her life on the line, and that mattered.

She'd never met anyone like Charli before. A woman who wore a hard shell for the world yet had lowered the screen to let Kayla inside her boundaries.

Kayla knew that nowadays many women played major roles in society, that they held positions of power and were respected by their peers. But in her experience, most of the females she'd encountered had been losers, blamed by their men for all the wrongs in the world.

As far back as she could remember, not one person, man or woman, had shown her any real kindness, other than an occasional social worker, and it was their job. She was just another kid on their long list of orphans, a responsibility... a chore.

The last worker, a motherly-type, had begged her to behave, to kick in and play the role she'd been given. Get her diploma so she could leave the system with something to benefit her – an education.

Those words had made sense in a time when nothing else had. She'd started to act out, make stupid choices, hang out with a gang destined to be in jail before their twentieth birthdays.

But Mrs. Hashill had talked with her, not down to her, gave her a dose of harsh reality. She'd made sense, words Kayla had needed to hear at that exact moment in time.

"Alicia, honey, listen to me. Hear what I'm telling you. I'm not sugar-coating it any longer – the time for that is long past. Instead, I'll tell you exactly what my husband told my son before he finally saw the light. No one truly gives a fuck about you. You understand?"

Hearing these words from the mouth of the middle-aged, motherly type got her attention.

"Yes, Ma'am."

"Don't "yes, ma'am" me, child. Most people only care about themselves. You don't even show up on their give-a-shit radar, unless you've got something they want."

"I know."

"No, you don't, girl. You're still pissed because you think the world owes you a good life, and you've been short-changed."

Unable to lie, Alicia had nodded.

"What you haven't figured out yet is this. Everyone is too busy worrying about their own shit. But, there is one person who truly cares and can do something about the mess you're in. You know who that is?"

Still feeling sorry for herself, tears escaping that she couldn't stop, Alicia shook her head. "No." The word came out low and with a sniffle.

"You. And if you're the only one you can depend on, then you better step up. *You* need to take over, be in charge, rather than let life play you. No matter what your circumstances, work the game in your favor. Get that education. You're smarter than most, Alicia, we both know it and that makes you lucky. You can be anything you want to be, because you do have choices."

Paying attention, she'd laid awake all that night replaying the words that made a wacky kind of sense. No one else gave a fuck, so she'd better start. From then on, she'd kicked in and brought her grades up. That had been the easy part.

Not making any waves, keeping her mouth shut... not so much. Living with the Whites had been a huge challenge. Thankfully, she'd had Buddy, who'd been the best part of that life. Over time, realizing she'd taken control, she'd begun to feel good about herself.

Until a sicko killer had shot holes through her chances, right in the forehead of a beautiful stranger. For a short while, she'd been in such despair, she'd thought again about ending everything, giving up completely.

Thankfully, she backed down, because now she had Charli in her life. Every time she thought about the Special Agent, how she'd jumped in to protect a stranger, how she accepted the role of babysitter for a teenager who had nothing, and how she'd hugged Kayla so gently, tears surfaced and Kayla dreamed.

Wouldn't it be wonderful to have a real sister like Charli, one to live with and be a part of her life? Someone who did give a fuck... really cared if she lived or died.

Someone *she* could love.

***

"The man keeps a nice house, but he certainly doesn't eat here very often. There's no real food here." Charli came out of the pantry with a package of noodles and a can of tomato sauce. "I guess I can rustle us up some spaghetti. So you won't be disappointed, Kayla, I suck at cooking. Gramps used to look after that part of our lives. He taught me how to cook a few meals, but I wasn't much interested."

"I can cook. I had no choice at some of the dumps they put me in; it was either cook or starve. What got me, there were others, smaller children who had no choice but to eat whatever garbage they put out. I began watching the cooking shows and picked up a few things. Even the Whites relied on me to make a lot of their meals."

"Then the job is yours." Charli handed over the can and noodle package and teasingly gave a yank on Kayla's long ponytail she'd gathered and wore in the front. "Tell me what you need, and I'll be your helper. I can set a mean table."

"Such accomplishments. I'm impressed," Kayla laughed.

"After supper, we need to go over the package again that Chief Prowler passed on."

"I've memorized it all, Charli. I'm even forcing myself to think Kayla rather than... ahhh, you know who."

"Good, kid. You're doing it right. But we still should perfect our stories because making a slip can be fatal. So... we'll eat and study." Charli watched the young girl searching for the tools she needed to prepare the meal, helped her find certain spices and picked up the remote control for the television in the corner, hanging from a stand over the table.

When the picture flashed; the grinning face of the man, who just that day she'd wished in hell, flashed on the screen. Kayla caught Blake's image and her excited exclamation stopped Charli from changing the channel... not that she would have.

The announcer spoke about an arrest that had happened a few hours earlier. A film started from where a wild-eyed culprit dashed out from between two parked cars, across the first lane to barrel into a car coming from the other direction.

It panned to where Blake followed from the same direction, flew over the hood, his ass sliding across like a scene in an action movie, just in time to overpower and arrest the protesting criminal.

TV high jinx!

"Local police Major keeping the streets of Fort Lauderdale safe... blah, blah, blah..."

Ratings slush!

"One more criminal safely behind bars thanks to our local law enforcement," the cooing announcer batted her eyelashes at Blake who hovered over her, looking bashful.

Give me a break!

"That's Blake. Look at the women watching him, everyone's taking pictures. He's so handsome, they love him. He's a hero."

Seriously? The man's a playboy posing as a cop.

Chapter Fifteen

Charli lay in the all-white, comfy, king-sized bed that night reviewing the day and the man who normally slept here. No matter how many times she pushed Blake Sebastian from her thoughts, her memory betrayed her, paying no attention to her aversion.

Sure, all right, so the man looked good in a uniform, most did. And he'd set them up in his beautiful house. He'd even agreed to give them their space and move into a hotel. Maybe the thoughtful gesture demanded some appreciation.

She didn't have to like the guy to take note of his kindness.

Grumpier now, she replayed the scene and felt better – she hadn't given him a lot of choices, had she? Therefore, he hadn't really been kind as much as he was in a tight spot and conceded.

Ha!

Truth was, she'd rather forced the issue – so he was still a hotshot hustler.

Should she feel like a shit for not being grateful enough to allow him to stay with them for added protection?

Not likely.

Being in such close proximity with that huge ego would have her climbing the walls and going for her gun. Better to keep him at a distance.

Plus, she had no doubt that she could keep them safe. No one knew where they were except for two people, Prowler and Crawly, and they would say nothing.

Their flight to Fort Lauderdale had been on a private plane the police used for these occasions. Rather than taking any chances of being seen at the Seattle airport, they'd driven to Vegas and caught the plane from there, hoping to mess with Dylan's ability to trace them. There would be no trail through the Seattle airport, other than from Melissa Dale, the agent who'd taken her original flight.

Flinging out her arms, and scissoring her legs against the smooth, fresh linen, Charli realized she felt safe. And it had been some time since she'd had the luxury.

Tomorrow, they had plans to work with Kayla on trying to find photos of Dylan in the databanks, in case he had earlier arrests. Barring that, the sketch artist would be arriving later to help her start reconstructing his face from memory, a memory that was fast fading according to Kayla.

For Charli, being that it was a weekday, she'd start Kayla's enrollment into the local school, get things in place for her to start the day after.

Then Charli would be briefed on producing the blog about editing they'd wanted her to use. It seems they had ways of making things online look as though they had been worked on for years; they just needed her presence there now.

Book editor!

Who the hell came up with that occupation? Charli, the woman who could barely put together a grocery list, now had to scribble online as if she had a successful career of editing a professional author's work.

Bah!

A grin took over, her better nature rose, and the humor of the joke kicked in. She shrugged and wished she could share this one with her Poppa John. He'd love the contradiction.

He'd often teased her that there was more to life than catching the bad guys. Maybe she should put as much energy into catching herself a good guy instead. Yeah, right! Like she needed more headaches!

She turned over, mashed her pillow and tried to make her muscles relax. Guess she shouldn't complain. She'd get her vacation, and if she didn't come up with material for the blog, they'd offered a backup professional who would write it for her.

Life couldn't be better, considering the circumstances. She began to doze off. Ooh, it felt so good to be safe.

Suddenly, a bright light flashed from the patio around the pool and seeped through the blinds.

What the hell? Someone had set off the outdoor overhead motion lights.

Chapter Sixteen

Hands shaking, Charli slowly eased from her bed and pulled her gun from the top drawer of the dresser where she'd stashed it before turning off the lamp. Sucking in deep breaths to calm her sudden frantic reaction, nerves now ramped up and giving her hell, she crept around the open door, and into Kayla's room.

Sneaking close to where the girl slept, she leaned forward. With her hand tight against Kayla's mouth, she swallowed hard to get her voice above a throaty whisper. "Kiddo, don't say a word. Someone's outside. Get into the bathroom and lock the door. Take your phone, and if I'm not back in a few minutes, call 911."

Even though the whites of her terrified eyes took over her small face, Kayla only nodded and followed orders. She palmed her phone and slid to the floor, crawling toward the open door of the bathroom. As soon as Charli heard the telltale click, she made her way toward an outside door.

Both bedrooms had side entrances to the patio, and she figured to sneak up and overpower the intruder rather than give him a clear view to take a shot if that's why he was there.

Once outside, using cover from the night-blooming, fragrant Jasmine shrubs, she held her gun steady with both hands and started forward. Feet bare, slithering on the damp grass after the sprinkler system had watered the yard, shivers crawled up her legs. She bit her lip to stop any noises escaping, like the moans that threatened.

Shit! You can do this, girl. It's a piece of cake after what you've been through recently. Calm down...

Heart beating crazy-like made her take in deep breaths through her nose and exhale through her mouth, a trick they'd taught at yoga classes to help clear one's mind and ease stress.

It worked. Calmer now, blessing her years of training, she moved forward. A stooped figure peeked into the patio doors. Whoever it was didn't seem to mind the lights, they were knocking against the glass as if paying a surprise visit. Then she heard a female voice and words that sounded like...

"Blake, baby, are you home?"

Stealing her way over the cement, sticking to the furniture that gave her some form of concealment, Charli got close enough to make out the body of a woman in a sheer, barely past her hips, wrap.

Charli called out in a no-nonsense voice, "Can I help you?"

Screams startled them both as the near-naked woman lost her cool, bellowed like a banshee and dropped a bottle of wine.

"Who are y-you?" Blonde and gorgeous, the woman stuck her hands up high which allowed her boobs to come pretty close to popping out of the skimpy covering.

"I think that's my question." Seeing no weapons, not any that could kill anyway, Charli lowered her gun and stepped forward into the light.

"No-o. I asked first." Hard voiced now, nasty Miss Peeping Tom demanded, "This is Blake Sebastian's house. Why are you here?" A dawning understanding began to form and the intruder's voice became ornerier. "Where is he? He send you out to protect him, the big baby?"

"No. He didn't send me out to protect him. He's not here. I'm staying in his house for a while, with my sister."

"Why would he let you stay here?" An angry frown formed as she spit out questions. "Are you his newest plaything? He changes them like most men change shoes. You know that, don't you? He's not a faithful man."

"Why are *you* here if he's such a shit?"

"Because. He's fun and a fantastic lover." Her manner still confrontational, she demanded, "You never answered my question." Her gaze travelled up Charli's baby-doll clad body and sneered at the normal-sized breasts pushing against the silky pale turquoise covering. "Why you?"

Blake's deep voice answered from the other side of the patio, where the tall garage gate, digitally password-locked, would have opened to allow only someone who knew the code entrance. "Because she's an old girlfriend from our collage days, and the only woman I ever gave an engagement ring to."

His husky voice sent tingles all through Charli's highly-strung body. She glanced at her prisoner, and her sense of humor kicked in. "For heaven's sake, blondie. Put your hands down. I'm not arresting you. Although I don't suggest you walk too far or you're liable to slip on the wine or get cut by the glass." She backed away with intentions to return to the house, then hesitated to see how Blake-baby would get himself out of this situation.

"Oh no, my goodness, look at this mess. Aww Blake, honey, I'm sorry. She scared the poop outta me, and I dropped my gift." Suddenly a little-girl's voice overrode the earlier woman's hard antagonistic tone.

Ignoring blondie, Blake stepped closer to Charli, his hand held out as if she needed to stop and let him speak. For a few seconds, tempted to ignore his command, she looked at the grass, but she waited.

"Kayla called it in. I was close."

"Very close. She must have just made the call." Charli searched his features and saw the devil's eyes narrow, as if he was thinking to invent an excuse. But he didn't and she had to give him credit for that.

"I'm sorry you were disturbed. Candy's my neighbor and I've ahh... she likes to surprise me...umm... we—"

"Listen bud, I don't care about what you, she or we... ahh, umm, do. Just call all your female friends, neighbors, the whole flippin' fan club and tell them your house is off limits, will you? Your Candy could have been hurt tonight."

"Yeah, Blake. She had a gun and was going to shoot me."

"She wouldn't have shot you, honey." Blake turned back to Charli. "You wouldn't have, right?"

Charli glared her answer, no smile to lighten the severity of the situation, although a grin hovered and was hard to hold back. "Might have. She's a sneaky intruder skulking around on private property."

"Blake-e!"

"She's joshin' you, Candy. But you should have called first, you know that, right?"

Whiny, Candy protested, "Then how could I surprise you?"

"Oh, for God's sake," Charli had had enough. "I'm going to get Kayla out of the bathroom, and we're going to bed." Before stomping away, she poked Blake in the chest. "You, clean up your ahh... mess."

***

"Kayla, it's me, Charli. It's safe to come out now." She knocked softly so as not to frighten the girl. "Kayla?" Twenty seconds passed, now Charli banged on the door with more force. "Kayla, are you okay, honey? Let me in."

Still more time elapsed before Charli finally heard the lock click, and the door open a few inches. Brown eyes, swimming in tears, streaks down both sides of her face, Kayla surveyed Charli and then let out a small sob. "Are you alone?"

Charli smothered her smile and answered seriously, "Yes, kiddo. The intruder was one of Blake's female neighbors come to visit."

"I heard screams and a crash."

"She dropped her bottle of wine after I snuck up on her. Blake arrived to help her clean up."

Kayla stepped into the open, her body still shaking. "Blake's here? I waited to hear the police sirens but nothing happened. I thought maybe the killer had overpowered you and was making you do what he said. Knowing you were out there all alone terrified me, Charli. It's such a huge risk."

"Get that crap out of your head, Kayla. The killer has no idea where we are. We're safe and as soon as the boys back home catch the asshole, we can go back and testify so he'll be put away for the rest of his life. That's the plan, right?"

Kayla's arms were crossed over her chest and her hands were rubbing the opposite shoulders. In a frayed, too-small nightie, the straps barely holding together, she looked scared, sick and exhausted.

Charli felt bad for her and softened her manner. "Come on, kid. Let's get you back to bed."

"Is Blake staying?"

"No. Why would he?"

"Because someone else could break in." Seeing the growing derision on Charli's face must have reminded her that she had protection... an FBI agent. "I'm sorry. You're here, I forget. But maybe he could be your back-up or whatever they call it. Do you think he would?"

Blake spoke from the entrance to the hallway. "Sure, Kayla, I'll sleep on the couch." He saw the fury Charli tried to hide and added, "Just for tonight so you girls can get some rest."

"Fine." Charli tried not to spit out the word... but to say it softly. Considering both of the others flinched and then quickly nodded, maybe she hadn't softened her tone as much as she'd thought she had.

Nevertheless, she'd had enough. "Come on, kiddo." She gave Kayla's long hair a playful pull and said, "I'll check the closet and under the bed. Will that satisfy you?" Teasingly, she put her arm around Kayla's shoulders and led the girl toward the bed. As they walked closer, Charli could feel the resistance inside the other girl.

At the bedside, she asked, "What's wrong, Kayla?"

"I'm scared. Did you know there's a door over there that leads outside?"

"Sure. There's one in my room, too. They're access to the patio. It's a nice idea, almost like having a balcony."

"But there's a huge window in the door and people can break through glass pretty easily. It's not very safe, don't you think?"

Charli softened. She remembered a time before her parents had passed, when she'd been scared to go back to her bedroom after a bird had flown into her window and killed itself. She'd mourned that bird, and when she lay alone, she couldn't seem to stop hearing the awful noise. Crying out, her father had arrived to pick her up, throw her over his shoulder and haul her into bed with him and her mother, to sleep between them.

"Feel better now, rascal?" he'd asked. And she had. So much so that she'd slept with them for days until her mother had put her foot down. From then on, her dad had slept on a pallet on the floor beside her bed.

Until one night, she'd seen him arch his back and moan, as if in pain. Guilt-ridden, she'd swallowed her fears and told him, "Go back to bed, Daddy. I'm not scared anymore." His words still resonated. "You're one brave little girl, Carolina my love. I'm proud of you." As if she was a General in an army, he'd saluted her and walked out, making sure the door was open and the hall light on.

Shit!

"You want to sleep with me, tonight, rascal? Just tonight, we're not making a habit here. But I need to get some rest and so do you. Stop bobbing your head like one of those dolls, it looks goofy. Okay, come on. Let's get some sleep."

Chapter Seventeen

Settling down on his long, plush gray sofa, a light fuzzy throw over his legs, Blake rubbed his hands together, still sticky from cleaning up the wine mess.

Whatever possessed Candy to drop by the one night he wished her on another planet? Sure, they'd had some fun times, and he'd let her in last week on one of the very few nights he'd stayed home to watch a game on TV.

They'd made out, had pizza delivered and gotten drunk from too much wine. But he'd made it clear; this wasn't to be a habit... just a one-time fling.

Hopefully, after the little session they'd had tonight where he'd told her that the one woman he'd ever truly loved was back in his life, and he meant to work at building a relationship with this ex-fiancee, she'd play-acted a few tears, wished him luck, and reminded him she only lived three doors down if things didn't work out.

All in all, she'd been a pretty good sport up until she left with the parting quip, "I expect a replacement for my bottle of wine. That shit cost me big bucks, Blake honey."

"Sure, Candy. I'll get it to you tomorrow. Thanks for understanding."

"Hell, dude, I just hope she's good enough for you. Seems to me she has a helluva long stick up her ass and a pissy attitude, too. But... if she's who you want, and there's no making sense of some guys' choices, then good luck."

Funny thing was – the real Charlotte, whose nickname had also been Charli, he'd known back in college had the same pissy attitude and had ignored him for the first few months of the semester. He'd had the hots for her, but whenever he'd approach, she'd give him a disdainful look, like he wasn't good enough for her to wipe her feet on.

Later he'd found out she had a boyfriend back home and was faithful to the promises she made to others.

Her boyfriend... not so much. After the Christmas vacation when she'd caught him playing around on her, she'd come back ready and willing to be friends with Blake. Good friends.

One thing she'd insisted on that surprised the hell outta him, she wanted to keep their affair a secret. "Are you ashamed of me?" He'd asked her, teasing, yet kind of serious, swallowing his hurt feelings.

She'd giggled in the cute way she had that made his heart trip all over itself and hugged him, "Are you kidding me? I'd be the envy of most of the girls who're making fools of themselves to get your attention. No, I'm not ashamed; just don't want to get caught up with those party animals you hang around with. I need to focus on my studies, okay?"

Who knows, maybe that ploy worked in her favor? Secrecy added spice and he'd fallen hard; even hit the point where he'd begun begging her to let him tell the world – "Charlotte Anglo's my girl." It wasn't allowed.

Okay, he'd admit the lying and sneaking had added an element of excitement to their fling, so much so that he'd fallen hard. Excited yet nervous, dressed in his best during one of their last dates before graduation, at a restaurant that would cost him a week's wage, bearing his heart in a small, silver-wrapped box sporting a fluffy, pink satin bow, he'd given her an engagement ring.

Her hesitation shocked him. "What are you doing?" Stunned, she'd whipped her hands behind her back and shook her head.

"I want us to get married. I figured we'd get hitched after our finals next month. I thought you'd be happy." By her actions, it was pretty fucking clear to him, she wasn't.

Not knowing how to handle rejection, his heart

broken, he'd tried to be the good guy, the understanding mate. So, he'd told her to keep his ring, take it with her when she went home for the Memorial weekend. Then, when she'd made up her mind, start wearing it.

Full of expectations that she would be showing it off the next time he saw her, especially after the passion they'd shared that night, the shock hit him hard. Not only *wasn't* she wearing his ring, she wore another's instead.

Seems his loving gift, the diamond he'd sweated and saved for over long months of working every job he could fit between his few hours a week with her and his classes, had pushed her old boyfriend into growing a pair.

The cheating bastard had apologized for his past behavior, promised fidelity and... gave her a solitaire too. Not one to brag, but it made Blake's look like the Krupp Diamond.

He'd learned well from that event. The so-called weaker sex – which was pure fallacy – could not be understood and never trusted. He should have known as soon as he'd seen the color of her hair. Carrot red and frizzy, like his mom, the nasty control freak his dad had put up with until he and his two siblings had left home, and the old man right behind them.

From then on, Blake disliked and distrusted red-headed women; stayed as far away from them as possible. Something about their mean temperament and cheating ways brought back bad memories.

He flipped his covers off and wriggled to find comfort. Just thinking about his mother made him twitchy, uncomfortable... with the urge to reach for the closest bottle. She'd been a real piece of work. Crabby on her good days and unbearable when she wasn't feeling good, which happened more often than not.

He'd left home at sixteen and never looked back, other than to connect with his brothers every so often and get the lowdown on his dad who lived alone in a trailer park somewhere in Florida. Old bastard deserved a decent retirement, peace and quiet from the harping and a few bucks in his pocket that he'd never had while living with her.

Those early traumatizing lessons had given him an insight into the twisted labyrinth of the minds of God's creation called Woman, and he'd never made the mistake of trying to get close to one of the strange creatures again.

Keeping his heart protected, he'd fooled around with them sure, but made his rules clear from the start. He'd give them as much enjoyment as he'd take. If the ladies offered, and they did a lot of offering, well what kind of a fool would turn them down? No male on the planet would blame him and very few women would either.

Very early on, he'd gotten a glimpse of the reality women live with, the almighty clinging to their youth; heaven forbid a wrinkle should appear, a rogue hair on a chin, or even worse – a pimple. OMG!! As the years passed, he'd noticed their penchant for clutching at their youthfulness with an increased desperation and that floored him.

Sure, men can be equally careful about their bodies. Watch their weight, some even have hair fetishes and go crazy on products that promise miracles. But in his experience, females were hands down bat-shit-crazy in their quest to stop the inevitable.

Strangely, Charli seemed not to care. He'd seen the way she controlled her curly hair with combs at the side or even bobby pins, like he'd seen his mom use back in the day. Not that it looked bad on Charli. Hell, quite the opposite. Her soft curls were bouncy and attractive.

The urge to pull one and watch it recoil had prompted him to piss her off at the airport, and the hunger to do it again haunted him.

He flipped over, unsettling thoughts disturbing his rest. Agitated, his mind revisited the shock he'd felt hearing Kayla's whispered 911 call for help. She'd eerily moaned Charli's name over and over, as if in a trance of terror for her make-believe sister.

Remembering his own ungodly fear, the stumbling when he'd rushed to get from his car, tripping, shaking, prayers uttered at the thought of their danger, he admitted to not having felt that kind of rookie trauma in a very long time.

No way would Blake admit to Charli that he'd been on the street sitting in his car, watching the house. It would infuriate her and undermine her confidence as an agent. He'd planned to stay until midnight when he had another officer detailed to take over the surveillance.

After reading the file on Dylan Ross, the infamous Silverado, there was no way he wanted the girls alone in the house. And the phone session he'd had with Deputy Chief Prowler, enlightening him to Charli's recent past, her undercover case, her exhaustion, meant he wouldn't be taking any chances that she'd be at her best, which he'd learned was better than most.

Then again, he'd originally planned on spending every night with the girls, and they'd have been covered. Well that went down like a defective bomb, didn't it?

Charli had crankily put the kybosh on that idea, and knowing they needed to have someone watching the place, he'd had to scramble for a replacement. After he'd called in to find out the men he could trust to keep their mouths shut about this place were covering a street concert downtown with a top headliner band, he decided the hell with it.

He'd take the first shift, and he'd call his Lieutenant, Bill Newton, to start at one a.m. at the latest. Bill was an Aussie who'd emigrated from Queensland five years earlier, a good man, one who owed him many favors.

With this guy, no explanations would be necessary. He knew the circumstances about the witness protection program, took orders, didn't ask questions and could be relied on to stay awake and do his job. He'd be arriving soon, then Blake could leave.

Nope! That wasn't going to happen either. He was exactly where he wanted to be.

Suddenly, still restless, he had the urge to check on the girls. Figured if he got caught, he'd use the excuse for needing the little boy's room. But he wouldn't be able to sleep now unless he knew for sure they were safe.

Sliding from the couch in his underwear, he slipped his pants back on and tiptoed to the first door in the hallway.

He peeked in and had the shock of his life. *What the hell?* The bed was empty. His head reeling with too many horrifying images whirling around, he crept closer and checked the other side in case Kayla happened to be a weird kid who slept on the floor. Nope! The room was empty.

Son of a bitch!

Moving quickly and in his haste, stubbing his toe, he clamped down on the cuss words, jogged awkwardly to the second door, and quiet as a burglar, he pushed down on the handle to open the door.

Moisture collected in his eyes at the beautiful

sight that awaited him and a soft mushiness invaded his whole being. The two girls lying together – Charlie with Kayla nestled against her side – slept like babies. He slinked closer, drawn by an invisible force, only to be met with the barrel of a gun inches out of the cover pointed directly at his heart.

Chapter Eighteen

Gesturing toward the hallway with the barrel of her weapon, Charli followed to ream him out. She'd tried to sleep but every sound the strange house produced had stopped that from happening. She'd only dozed and the results were that she felt jumpy and mean.

"What in the name of all that's holy possessed you to come into our room. I was seconds away from blowing the top of your head off."

"Actually, you were aiming at my heart."

"Pure semantics, my dear Watson."

"Aha! Quoting Sherlock Holmes, you can't be that mad."

"I never get mad. But I hate things that don't make sense. You, Watson, you don't make sense."

"So you hate me?"

"Now you're just being an ass. And you're quibbling... answer my question."

"I couldn't sleep and decided to check on you ladies. When I found Kayla missing – trust me – it took a few years off my life. I had to make sure she was with you before calling in the troops, didn't I?"

"When you put it that way, it makes sense. Okay. I would have done the same."

"So, does that mean you can put your gun down now?"

Charli's eyes had settled on his naked chest and for some ungodly reason, her hands wanted to follow, to search those strong lines, the muscles, his nipples, to caress and stroke. *Charli, he's asking you something!* "Ahh... pardon me?" The glint in his knowing eyes, his cocky grin and his husky teasing stiffened her resolve and got her mind back on track. "What?"

"Put your gun down. You're pointing it at me again."

Sure enough, she now had it aimed right at his groin, and it pleased her to see the cockiness he'd worn a few seconds earlier had disappeared. "Sorry." She lowered her arm. Realizing her silky pajama top was no cover at all from his prying eyes, she turned to go back inside. "Goodnight."

"Do they always bounce?"

What? "Does what always bounce?" Her mind in the gutter thinking he was talking about her chest, she itched to aim her weapon once more so he'd start behaving.

"Your golden curls. They bounce."

Why she turned back to face him, she'd never know.

He reached out and tugged at the one draped over her forehead, the same bunch she constantly had to pin up to keep out of her eyes.

The very gentle way he handled it, kind of like her Poppa John often did when he wanted to make a point and get her to listen; it wrenched her heart from its hidden shelter and left it unprotected, accessible, searching for proof that here was a person it needed to bond with.

Good God, no!

Before she could wrench away, he'd lowered his lips and kissed the golden locks in his fingers. His manly smell filled her nostrils and his body heat titillated her own body to accept, to move closer... to investigate.

Sucking in her breath, she froze. Again, why she didn't stop his nonsense kept her awake the rest of the night, but the intrigued female entity inside refused to let this moment pass without experiencing it fully.

His nose pushed at the hair on her forehead as he kissed there, too. Then he made his way to her ears while his hands cradled her face. "Charli, girl, I have no idea why, but those curls do things to me, give me very ungentlemanly feelings. So, before we both end up in that empty bedroom Kayla abandoned, I believe you need to stop me now."

She didn't move, couldn't. His voice had put her

in a trance. The husky, sexy tones had her quaking with needs she'd kept tamped down for a very long time.

He moaned. His lips moved to hers and were descending, his hot breath close while the sweep of his long eyelashes brushed her cheek. For just a second, she savored the feel of his soft mouth against hers, and then she lifted the gun and dug it into his side.

He backed off, her message clear. But his husky muttering left her shaken to the core, "Oh, baby, you know you're gonna be mine."

Chapter Nineteen

Charli couldn't believe how the weeks sped by. She missed her grandfather, Poppa John, with a vengeance and had to stop herself from trying to find a way to contact him. But there was none. He was too precious to endanger, and in case Silverado had connected her to the night of the shooting – no sign yet that he had – then they needed to be on extra alert with her only family.

The lodge staff had been given strict orders that if they saw anyone who didn't belong near John Madison, they were to contact Detective Crawly immediately. By all the reports Blake passed on – his thoughtfulness a nice surprise – things seemed quiet back home, and Charli could breathe easy.

Here in Fort Lauderdale, she spent the days resting or pretending to work on her fictitious blogs, which usually started off with some inane drivel no one could decipher. Then, with a smirk at her own inept silliness, she'd pass them on to the expert, Suzanne F, to totally redo before she'd post them.

And... she helped Kayla get assimilated into the nearby High School. The girl was woefully lacking the normal teenage necessities. Rushing, they bought her school supplies, a new phone and personal oddities like makeup and toiletries.

Next, Kayla's wardrobe depressed Charli to the point that she used her own money to outfit the kid with some decent, modern shit: jeans, tops and underwear that fit.

Almost comatose from excitement by the end of the shopping trip, Kayla had finally put a stop to Charli's spending. "No more, Charli. I love everything, but you've gone overboard. Besides, I don't trust you when you say the budget covers all this stuff. You can't make me believe the Government's this generous."

But the glow in Kayla's sparkling browns spurred her on.

"Just a few more things. Come on, kiddo. You need a couple of bathing suits and shoes, right? I love shopping for shoes."

By the time Charli ran out of wind, they'd hit most of the stores in the Galleria Mall and were loaded with shopping bags. She hadn't expected to have so much fun spending her money, it hadn't happened in a long time, and seeing Kayla's excitement, her joy and disbelief in everything they chose made it worth every penny.

The evenings were relaxing and exactly what Charli needed. She and Kayla worked out together: yoga, defense lessons and taking turns exercising on the various machines Blake had chosen to outfit his private gym.

Other than the nightly drop-ins from Blake, who teased the teenager outrageously until they both dissolved into fits of laughter – Charli hiding her grins – the two females hit a plateau where they fit comfortably.

Charli admitted that Kayla was the more easy-going of the two and smoothed any friction between Blake and her with a well-placed quip. Her personality had blossomed from a girl used to keeping her thoughts to herself, to a happy-go-lucky teen, building confidence that pleased Charli every time she could see the new Kayla stepping forward, putting it out there... taking a chance.

After dropping Kayla off at school and maybe grabbing a few needed groceries, Charli would spend her mornings reading and snoozing by the glorious pool. The refrain that echoed daily – *What a life!* – was instrumental in her nerves relaxing their steel-like restraints and her changing sleep habits.

Now that Kayla slept in her own bed again, thanks to Charli's offering to put baby monitors in their rooms so they'd be in instant communication, the nights weren't near as restless. She'd managed to cut down her house inspections spurred on by random noises to only one or two a night.

The one bone of contention she had with their routine were the nightly visits from Blake, but because he'd pass on different messages to her from Crawly, who'd begun to drop by to see her grandfather every few days, she kept her mouth shut and just made sure they were never alone.

Instead, she watched him from afar, careful never to come into physical contact and continued to relive their breathless, electrifying... almost kiss.

Last night, he'd passed on what the middle-aged cop told him. That what had started out as part of Crawly's job had become an activity he looked forward to, spending time with old-man Madison. Seems the men, both widowers, had hit it off, and Crawly enjoyed John's witty, dry humor, the odd game of Shuffleboard and wine with her gramps by the pool at the lodge, one of her favorite pastimes, too.

Considering her gramps only had vision in one eye, and even that was slowly deteriorating to peripheral, he managed to play those Shuffleboard rocks well enough to have beaten her many times. Not that he'd boast about winning unless you could call a loud WOOWIE with a fierce high-five, a small dance and grins from ear to ear crowing. *Yeah, right!*

Crawly had passed on a "John" story to Blake that still had him snickering, and Charli comically shaking her head when he'd shared it with her.

The men were in John's apartment, and two of the young, pretty caregivers working at the lodge had stopped by to deliver John a blister pack with his daily pill – one pill mind you – ninety years old and only a blood thinner. He liked to mention that to her as often as... every freakin' single time she saw him. Warmth spread through Charli and she missed her gramps so much it hurt.

She knew why the girls came. Sure, they had to deliver his pill, but he was a favorite, and they liked to fuss over him, to offer assistance in case he needed help at bedtime.

Blake continued, "Seems they gave a quick knock and entered the room. Then your gramps had looked at Crawly, winked and asked him, *"Which one do you want?"* Crawly said the girls just giggled and smacked the older man gently while shushing him. John grinned at them, but in an aside to Crawly, he retorted, *"They think I'm kidding."* It took longer than it should have for Crawly to finish telling me this, but he kept cracking up before he could get the story out."

Charli could tell by the way Blake talked that he'd gotten a huge kick out of the tale.

Still enjoying the humor of the story, Blake laughingly admitted, "I'd sure like to meet your grandfather. He sounds like a real character."

"Me, too, Charli." Kayla had sat entranced and had laughed uproariously at the old man's antics.

"Oh, he is. Most of his life he worked on engines, in car garages in his earlier years, which kept him, Grandma and their kids, my mother being one of them, poor as church mice. Then he moved on, took a diesel mechanics course by working his regular ten hour days and studying late at night. My mom used to tell me how she'd come out to the kitchen in the middle of the night for a drink and find him passed out over his books at the table. After my parents were killed when I was ten, I moved in with them. By then, he'd been working in the mines where he did quite well, became a foreman, and his wages improved."

"Did he work underground?"

"Of course, right at the face. He specialized in what he used to call the Moving Carpet where he fixed drills and all kinds of heavy-duty equipment."

"Man... that had to be a hard life."

"Especially hard on his body. After he retired, he went back to school to be retrained – in food preparation of all things. Him, sixty-two-years-old, and nineteen others in their late teens and early twenties, who all adored him. He then worked as a breakfast cook at a restaurant in town. Finally, the long hours of standing got to be too much, and my grandma put her foot down, made him quit."

Kayla, entranced by the story, kicked in, "He must be a very special person."

"You'd love him. But wait, there's more. Next,

he went to two stained glass classes and picked up the basics. After a lot of reading and a bit of trial and error, he spread his work everywhere. Back home, I have lamps, vases, jewelry boxes, window ornaments and the most breathtaking Christmas village you'll ever see."

Blake piped up, "Stained glass. Now that I never saw coming! So, he's creative too."

"Strangely creative, who knows what he could have been if he hadn't lost his own dad at thirteen and been forced to work. Back in those days, it's what one did. He had a mom and three siblings to help take care of. That's when he taught himself about engines, and it gave him a way to make a living with only a fourth grade education."

"No wonder he made the most of his retirement. He finally had a chance to do something he loved," Blake surmised.

"True. He told me he couldn't afford to do it in the style he'd have preferred. For instance, he did a bit of carpentry before the stained glass but he didn't have the right tools and a large enough shop. But he managed to renovate their house and build some tables and a china cabinet for Grandma, which he still has today."

"Wow, it hasn't been easy for him. Makes me realize I'm not the only kid who has obstacles," Kayla shook her head.

"I think a lot of our oldies had far more to handle than some of us realized. He finally had to stop both his hobbies, and it wasn't because he lost the sight from his one eye, but because they'd moved to the lodge and there was no room for him to set up shop. At first, he missed it terribly, until I finally stumbled on audio books as a way for him to fill those hours. After Grandma passed last year, he needed something he could focus on and between his activities at the lodge, listening to his favorite suspense authors and all the visitors he gets, life isn't too bad for him. At least he's happy, as you can tell by his quirky sense of what's funny."

Looking back, it still shocked Charli at how much she'd shared about her grandfather and their personal business that evening. It wasn't a normal way for her to behave, but then it wasn't normal for her to be completely separated from him for such a long time either.

Lordy, how she missed spending time with him. All through her last undercover stint, what kept her going was constantly revisiting her plans for them to be together on a vacation.

If only he was here now, enjoying this house and pool with her like they'd planned. She glanced around at the gleaming white walls, the blue and yellow ceramics inside the pool area and the plush royal blue furnishings. She suffered a long breath full of sorrowful disappointment.

If only...

Restless now, she remembered that today she didn't have chauffer detail. Seems that Kayla had made a new friend almost upon starting her first class, and the two girls would be stopping at the mall after school, a teenage girl's favorite pastime. Then they planned to come home by bus, followed, of course, by an undercover cop that Blake assigned to tail them as soon as he'd heard their plans.

Last night before bed, Kayla had opened the conversation yet again. "Are you sure you don't mind Angie coming for supper and a sleepover, Charli?" Kayla stood at the bathroom sink, washing a bright turquoise blouse, one of her new ones.

"Why would I mind? I'm glad you made a friend. And why are you washing that in the sink instead of the washer?"

Kayla shyly admitted, "It's so bright; I was worried the color would run and look, it did."

Joking, Charli pretended to reach outside the door and wrestle with a phantom. "Gotcha, you bastard! Get back here."

Brows arched in confusion, Kayla questioned, "What are you doing?"

"I caught that sucker running, put up one hell of a fight."

Laughing hard, Kayla's howls finally turning to snickers, she snorted, "You're nuts!"

Charli winked and watched the girl in the mirror over the sink. Most of the shadows around her beautiful, dark Chinese eyes had thankfully faded.

But then a worried look reappeared.

"What?"

"You're sure it's okay for me to be out in public?"

"Of course, why are you fussing?" For a few seconds, Charli felt the same anxiety, but shook it off.

"I got the feeling you hesitated when you said I was allowed to go."

"Sure, because I haven't met your friend, Angie, yet. As for the other, it's been weeks now and no sign of Long John Silver, so I'm breathing a bit easier."

Laughing at Charli's nickname for a man as dangerous as her stalker, Kayla wouldn't stop gnawing at the proverbial bone between her teeth. "You're sure? We could head straight here, instead."

"If it'll make you feel less nervous, and to be on the safe side, Blake promised to have one of his people shadow you at the mall. If they're good at their job, you won't even know they're around. So, you go and have some fun, make sure you take the money I gave you and spend it. Time you felt like a normal kid. Soon enough, when they catch that slime ball, we'll be back into that whole mess again. I'd like to think this time here in witness protection with me wasn't all turmoil and worry."

Kayla turned to Charli and the look on her face gave Charli warning. *The kid needs another hug... again!* Her charge had become fond of cuddles, so much so that Charli had to suffer them frequently. It was as if Kayla had been starved of affection for so long that she intended to make up for that lack all at once.

Bracing herself, not giving any indication that this was hard for her, she gathered the girl close and let her hand smooth the long black hair. A few seconds was all that was needed, and Kayla pulled back. "So, you really don't mind. I'll be home in time to make supper, I promise. And you're sure that Angie can spend the night?"

"For the seventeenth time, no problem." Charli teasingly rolled her eyes, dropped her chin to her chest and sighed loudly. When she peeked up to see Kayla's brightness, she changed the subject. "First of all, I'm ordering pizza for a treat. And second, tell me more about your friend."

"I already told you most of what I know. She lives in that residential area, can't remember the name, it's on the other side of the school, with her sick mom and a stepdad. Her older brother and sister left last year because of him... couldn't stand being around him, I guess. If the look in her eyes when she talks about him is any indication and her calling him a sick, slimy bastard helps, I'm pretty sure she hates him, too."

"Poor kid."

"I know, and I thought I had it bad. She hasn't said much more about him but her eyes speak for themselves. He must be horrible." Kayla hesitated, but then continued, "She kinda dresses like a middle finger against tradition too. She told me her hair used to be down to her hips last year but she cut it all off and changed her look. Piercings and her hair is wild, all uneven and colored often pink or purple.

"She has a lot of tight clothes torn in strategic places, like some of the stuff you see in the stores today. But my belief is they're just old and too small on her, so she covers that up by ripping them.

"One thing is for sure, she's smart, more so than me, and as you know, I'm no slouch. She challenged me on a math test, and I figured ninety-eight percent would trump her, but she got a hundred. Shocked the math teacher, you know the stickler I told you about, Mrs. Moore, who rides her all the time, says she's wasting her potential. Well, she proved it that day."

Charli was intrigued. Now she looked forward to meeting this girl even more.

Chapter
Twenty

John Madison missed his little girl, not that she was still little... or a girl. All woman and an FBI agent, Charli would always be his precious baby granddaughter. And they had a routine he happened to cherish.

But it had been a long time, almost two weeks, since she'd contacted him. That had never happened before. She'd always managed to call every few days, even when she was undercover. He missed hearing her voice teasing him with her usual opening line, "Hey Popsicle. How's things?"

The fact that she hadn't called this time, even though she'd warned him she couldn't, gave him even more reason to worry. After a couple of glasses of wine to loosen the man's tongue, he'd set up traps to pry information from Mark Crawly. From his careful answers, John surmised that Charli'd taken on a witness protection gig. At least, that's what he'd guessed and Crawly hadn't refuted it, just changed the subject.

Having listened to a lot of audio suspense books and watched a lot of his favorite cop shows on TV, he decided to follow up on his instincts. He took one of the younger lodgers, a guy in his late seventies, aside. "Brad, you used to be an editor for one of the big newspapers, right?"

"Yep, those were the fun days, before my heart attack. Now, I'm just getting over my pneumonia, and still dealing with my Plantar Fasciitis and that makes walking as painful as hell."

Thinking to butter him up, and against his better judgement because he knew the man to be a boring, whining hypochondriac whose every ailment became solely his own property, he dutifully said, "Sorry to hear that, Brad. You better now?"

"Better than my doctor."

"Why? What do you mean?"

"Well, a week ago I went to see him, and he said I had pneumonia. Told me we had to be careful because it killed old people like me."

"Guess you beat it?"

"I did, but when I went back to see my doc earlier this morning, the nurse said he'd died yesterday... from pneumonia. Shook me up, I tell ya."

John hid a grin. "How old was he?"

"Oh, just a youngster, maybe fifty. A pity."

At Brad's reply, John broke down and he

laughed until he noticed Brad didn't get the joke. His sour expression warned John to get serious. "So, what do you need to see me about?"

John sobered, not wanting to put Brad in one of his moods. "If I wanted to look up a certain day on the internet, involving stories about police activities, what's the easiest way?"

Brad's features became all business-like. "You mean ordinary break-ins and thefts or felony criminal cases like murder?"

"I'm thinking the bad shit. Can you show me?"

"All you'll get from newspapers is what the police have offered to the reporters, not any in-depth explanations. You know that, right?"

"Sure, sure. I'm thinking something happened the night or two before Charli took off, and she's involved in some way. I'm just being nosy."

"Okay, it'll be easy. And if you want more, I can always call in a few favors from the guys I know who still work at the paper."

Soon, they sat together at his desk while Brad's still limber fingers worked magic with the keys on his laptop. Together, they searched various newspapers and went back to the last few nights that Charli had been in town. Brad filtered through all the police posts and tragedies that took place in Seattle and eventually they hit the mother-load. They found what they sensed might be *the* story.

A woman in an apartment across from Charli's

had been found shot, and there were no suspects yet. Which had to mean that the killer was still on the loose. Maybe someone had witnessed the shooting and could identify him? That's if this story ran along the same lines as one of the old cop series, *In Plain Sight*, John had faithfully watched a few years ago.

Every week, they'd have to protect a witness, and so they'd moved him/her away until the killer was taken into custody. On one show that stood out in his memory, they'd intended to hold a trial so the witness could put the killer away for good. Except that's not what happened.

The killer had found the victim's family and taken them hostage. When the witness learned the truth, through social media leaking the story, he'd slipped away from his protectors to save his wife and child. If John remembered correctly, this had led to a huge battle where, of course, the law had arrived in time to shoot the killer. Other than the witness getting shot in the arm, the law had prevailed.

Great! He liked an ending where the good guys won – maybe because he was ferociously proud of his Charli and the role she'd chosen as an FBI agent, to help others and uphold the law.

"Hey, John, is this enough for now? Its dinnertime and they're serving stuffed chicken breasts tonight. You know, I need to keep my strength up."

"No problem, you go ahead. And, thanks, Brad. You've been a big help." He fetched Brad's walker that had been moved to the side.

Once Brad had his wheels, he left John to ponder over what they'd found. So, if Charli was involved in something like this, where would she go? Would they give her a choice? If he knew his Charli, he'd bet the farm she'd opted for Fort Lauderdale. Would they allow the protector to choose their own hiding place?

Damned if he knew the answer.

Suddenly, he hurried to his night table and found the printouts of the house Charli had rented for them for their vacation in Fort Lauderdale.

Maybe he could find out.

He quickly rushed to the desk and checked on his laptop to see if the house was available for the month that Charli had booked it. Now that she had a case, he figured she'd have canceled the agreement and gotten a refund... wouldn't she?

Could the rental agency find another interested party for the expensive house on such short notice? He wouldn't think so. It should show as available.

Hell. It wasn't. Either they had found occupants, she hadn't canceled... or what if she was there? Would the authorities allow Charli to use that particular place for her witness? After all, the house in Fort Lauderdale had already been rented under her own name.

But... in witness protection, the subjects would be forced to change their names. So, couldn't they show the changed names on the rental agreement now? Therefore, the trail would be cold. Hmmm... would the authorities let that happen?

He wasn't sure, but one thing he did know, the house sat on a lagoon he was familiar with. Surveying the printout again, seeing the buildings in the background, he knew that area well. Could he find that particular house? Sure, easy-peasy. He'd rent a boat and go up and down the Intracoastal Waterway until he recognized the yard he saw in the photo, the one where the owners had put a stained glass insert in the upstairs window. That alone was like a sign.

But would Charli be happy to see him? He grimaced. He'd never interfered with her job before. He had to think carefully about this.

Would the cops be pissed if he slipped away? Who cares! Well, except for Mark Crawly... he'd become a good friend.

Should that stop him? Aw, crumbs. He was too old for this shit. On the other hand, at ninety, life was too short for him to waste another week without his kiddo. He'd think hard.

Chapter
Twenty-one

After the hilarious pizza fest with Kayla and Angie, thanks to Blake's constant teasing and jokes, Charli let him help clean the kitchen so he'd stick around. Uneasy, she had to share her feelings and intended to discuss her apprehension with him.

Before she could open the conversation, Kayla returned, Angie trailing behind her. "Charli, do you have an extra bathing suit Angie could borrow. Mine won't fit her."

Cutting off Charli's response, Angie's agitation clear, she said, "No biggie, Kayla. I told you, I can wear my shorts and t-shirt." She pulled on Kayla's arm, but did so gently.

Ignoring the other girl's discomfort, Charli answered the question, "Sure, kiddo. I washed all three of mine and left them hanging in my bathroom." She smiled at Angie, watching the sullen expression transform into pleased shock.

"Angie, take whichever one you want."

"Thanks, Charli, you're aces." Kayla beamed with gratitude and Angie just looked like a victim who'd taken a two-by-four to the head. It made Charli wonder how often the girl made requests and had them granted.

After they headed to the pool, Charli shared her fears with Blake.

"Can I talk to you about this new girl, Angie?"

"Sure." He leaned against the counter, crossed his arms and waited.

She folded the towel and hopped onto the counter opposite him. Watching him, watching her, as she took her comb out of her hair, used it to gather the curls by her ears that had escaped and replace it, she ignored the flash of interest he didn't attempt to hide and began.

"When the girls first arrived home, things were definitely awkward. Angie was offhand to the point of being unapproachable. No matter what I said, the girl couldn't seem to relax. I thought if I asked questions, it might be easier for her, but her answers were noncommittal to the point of rudeness."

"You probably interrogated the poor baby."

"That poor *baby*, as you call her, sports 38 D's and has eyes that said goodbye to innocence a long time ago."

Being used to such insolent attitudes in her undercover work with young gang members,

Charli had sensed an underlying reason for Angie's reticence. Just the girl's appearance screamed abhorrence with rules of normal behavior. Then she remembered what Kayla had told her about the girl, about her dysfunctional family.

"Kayla told me earlier she had an asshole for a stepdad, her siblings escaped last year, leaving her there alone, and her mom being ill doesn't help the situation."

"There's no law against having a broken family, Charli, my love. Sadly, it's now the norm in many areas. She seemed nice enough with Kayla, almost worshipping in a way."

Charli sneered at his cheeky "my love" endearment, which just made him grin, but his comment made her rethink the situation. "You're right. As snarly as she was with me, she behaved completely the opposite with Kayla."

"See, that's what I noticed. Two friendly, even affectionate, girls behaving the way young teenagers do who've lacked their family's attention."

Charli gaped at the man beside her. "And you know that how?"

"I spend a lot of my spare time at the gym and work out with the kids. Most seasons, I teach defensive training classes for a mixed group of middle-aged gems. I get to see a lot of interaction, and I'd say a lot of Angie's reserve is because she's been trained to be seen and not heard."

"So, she makes sure that what you see is outrageous and shocking, her way of saying screw you." That made a lot of sense. Charli looked toward the patio, through the sliding glass doors and saw the girls standing together, holding hands, ready to dive in. Straggly pink spikes contrasted to Kayla's black hair... one bright sunrise, the other dark night.

Angie, cute and short, beside Kayla's longer, slender body caught the eye. And the differences in their dress code had stuck out too.

On purpose, Charli had allowed Kayla full choice when they'd shopped, and the girl had a natural chic that had her picking classier outfits rather than garishly modern. Not so for Angie. Her jeans had so many rips across the front that most of her tanned legs were on display all the way up to her crotch.

Oh stop fretting like an old mother hen. Opposites attract – it's a slogan because it's true.

Changing the subject, Charli turned to Blake who'd moved to stand nearby. "Truthfully, most nights I dread you showing up, uninvited I may add, but tonight your shenanigans – teasing the girls and telling those crazy stories – helped everyone relax. Thank you for that."

"Aww Charli, you know I have to come to get a change of clothes and check in. Besides, I'd miss your sweetness if I skipped a night. I even had you laughing earlier. Admit it, you like having me here."

"I liked seeing Angie let loose, even though she is flirtatious to a fault. Man, she's only fourteen. I bet I never acted like that."

"Whoa-ho. I'd put my money on it." His teasing grin made her laugh. She jumped down and pushed him in a friendly way, but with a warning he couldn't ignore. He'd let his body brush up against hers too often to be coincidental. The room was just not that small. "Stop it."

"Stop what?"

"You know."

"Nope."

"Do so."

He laughed. "All I know is this is one of the weirdest conversations we've had, and there've been some doozies."

"Stop rubbing against me." He'd purposely done so again, and she pushed harder, only this time he didn't move.

"You think I'm doing it on purpose? Honey if I wanted to get close to you, I'd just do this." He whipped her around before she escaped, his arms gathering her in close. Hungrily, he growled a groan that resonated throughout her body, igniting every cell from the top of her curly head to the tips of her pink-painted toenails.

She shoved against his chest with a lackadaisical effort he totally ignored. "Stop, you're being a pest."

His hands moved to her face, his palms warm and gentle. "No." He kissed her forehead first and rubbed his nose against hers.

If he'd tried any other kind of foreplay, forced himself on her in any way, her defenses would have kicked in. He'd have found himself writhing on the ground.

But the crafty bastard must have sensed that her one weakness was a gentle hand, a sweet kiss... a meaningful murmur. Frozen, she closed her eyes and allowed the seduction to continue.

Waiting for his lips to finally capture hers, she experienced passionate participation in her lower body. Muscles clenched enticingly. Signals of arousing spasms slithered to attack her mushy brain. And while her legs turned to sticks of jelly, a damp welcoming oozed from the throbbing area between them that begged for attention.

Before she could plead for mercy, to give her what her whole being craved, sanity returned, and she wrenched away. "Stop it! Go find one of your Candy's to play with. I'm not your type."

Silence boomed. Would he react badly? Or accept her rejection? She waited, fearing she might have pushed him too far.

Bending, hiding his arousal by leaning against the island, his tone held no anger. Instead he teased, murmuring in a husky voice, "A fellow gets kinda sick of all that meaningless sugar. After a while, he needs some sour in his life to offset so much sweetness."

The crafty bastard had her. No way she'd respond.

Again silence reverberated. This time it appeared less tense.

He broke it first. "So, did the girls have fun at the mall today?"

"Yes, they mentioned it at dinner, which, unsurprisingly, you arrived for just in time."

"Must have been before I got here. And I did bring dessert. You know, Kayla invited me yesterday, wanted me here to share the meal. Didn't she tell you? She asked me so I could meet her new friend."

"No, she never mentioned it." Her vexation appearing once again, she grumbled, "Stop trying to hold my hand." Charli yanked the object under discussion away from him. "I have a feeling you put the words in her mouth, something you're good at I noticed."

"Ah! You notice me. I'm flattered."

Groaning, Charli pointed her finger in his face. "See, there you go again; defining things in such a way you know aren't true." After he kissed her finger, she looked up as if praying for tolerance. "Stop that."

"Stop what? Wanting you? Can't do that. I'd have to quit breathing first."

"Okay. That works for me." She threw him an evil grin and put the counter between them.

Becoming serious, and changing the subject back to what bothered her most, she added, "Did you pick up any strange vibes from Angie?"

"You mean like she's a flirt?"

"Not just that. I must say, though, you handled her obvious eyelash-batting very well... and without embarrassing her." Once spoken, Charli had to admit the truth of her words. Blake had been kind, even gentle with the girl's ploys that left no awkwardness.

"Wow, a compliment!" His green bewitchers caught and held hers until her heartbeats tripled, and her hands began to tremble. *Damn stress. He just has to look at me, and I'm a mad mess.*

Needing the upper hand again, she spoke and dissipated the magic, "Angie has obvious baggage, and I'm worried about Kayla getting caught up in it. She's fragile."

"I don't see that. I see a strong sense of right and wrong and a huge heart undamaged by her past. Gotta tell you, I'm beginning to care about that girl one hell of a lot more than I should. I'm thinking to stay in her world after all this nonsense has passed. Figure she'll need friends, and I can be a good friend, it's something you don't know about me."

Shocked, she asked, "You mean you'll adopt her?" She scoffed. "Like the courts will allow a bachelor like you to take on the care of a girl her age?"

He stiffened. "I didn't say adopt, though it's a thought. And you seem to have a slightly skewed impression of my reputation in Fort Lauderdale. I'm a respected Major, and the many years that led to me attaining this level were spent serving the public. So you know; I'm held in high regard throughout this area."

Suddenly, the playboy faded and Charli faced the man behind the badge, the professional who'd earned the right to supervise a large department. This man had charisma, sure, because of his handsome face and well-formed physique, but more importantly, he had a no-nonsense manner that anyone faced with his powerful presence would respect and obey.

He interrupted her unsettling reflection. "I'm becoming very fond of Kayla. I'd hate to see her being returned to the system."

Backing off, her respect for the man taking a sudden upward curve, she changed the subject. "Is there any word on Dylan Ross?"

"The trail is as cold as my favorite maple-walnut ice cream. Interpol's now involved, along with all the local agencies where he's managed to make a kill and get away. No one's had any sightings. I've got a file so big it's overflowing, yet there's nothing concrete we can check. It's frustrating as hell."

Charli felt her nerves begin to react. "That son of a bitch is a menace. Look, there's no doubt he'd be after a witness who can ID him. He's gotta be trying to find out where Kayla's hiding."

"I know. It's eerie. Other than a mass shooting in the industrial section near the airport yesterday that caught my attention, nothing's happened out of the norm."

"A mass shooting? Was it a professional job?"

"It had all the markings. The cold-blooded shooter eliminated three men in a bar, but it made no sense."

Blake's perplexing comment urged Charli to request more details. "What happened?"

"Well, this guy walked into Freddie's, a kind of honky-tonk hangout for bikers, and shot three people. The only thing tying the massacre to your case was that all three bullets were targeted in the forehead."

"Any witnesses?"

"One man, an accountant-type doing the books in the back for free drinks, didn't see anything, he only heard the shots."

"And, no doubt, dove for cover."

"Seems to be the case. Says he hid in the closet they use as a filing cabinet until he knew the coast was clear. Then he called 9-1-1."

"And he had no idea why these people were killed?"

"Nope. But he admitted that Freddie, the bigot who owned the pub, made enemies from being a racist prick who'd often tell people he didn't want to serve to fuck off. His guess was that the killer could have been a black man who didn't take kindly to being called names and told to leave."

"A black man?"

"That's what he figures."

"Well, shit!"

Chapter Twenty-two

After the house settled, Blake collected clean clothes and left. The girls finally settled in Kayla's room. And, Charli lay in her bed, her suspense novel thrown aside. She couldn't concentrate. All she could think about was the incident Blake described just before he'd said goodnight.

A black man executed three others. Could that be their killer? Could he have reached Fort Lauderdale because he knew Kayla was close? Should they move on somewhere else?

She'd asked Blake the same questions but he'd said to give it a couple of days. They were still hot on this killer's trail, checking all the videos they could gather from around the isolated bar, interrogating their useless witness in case he'd missed something, and working the crime scene for any evidence.

Unsettled, she rose to do one last walk around

the inside of the house, checked all the windows, tightened the latches and double-checked to be sure the security system was activated and the screens were clear.

Then she returned to her room, slid back into bed and turned on the baby monitor as per her nightly routine.

Settling under the covers, she suddenly remembered their visitor and reached to turn it off. Surely Kayla wouldn't have bothered using it tonight. Then she realized the girl had forgotten... or had she? Hearing Angie's words froze her hand in midair, and she listened. Any rights to privacy vanished after she heard the first few words.

"Look at this palace. Compared to you, I live in a shitty world, Kayla. I used to plan my death, like, you know, a celebration. Eat my last dinner of steak and ice cream. Then cut off all my hair and leave a note for the authorities to give it to some poor cancer victim. Ask them to pass on my body parts to those sick people who really want to live. And then take a handful of opioids, those fucking pills my mom gobbles down that turns her into a useless blob."

Agitated, her voice full of tears, Kayla's whimpers of pity tore Charli apart. Eyes full after hearing Angie's heart-wrenching statement, she'd had to cover her mouth so her reaction wouldn't tip off the girls that they had an eavesdropper. Completely mesmerized, she continued to listen.

"Angie, you can't do that. Please, please don't. We're friends now, you're not alone anymore."

"Man, I still can't believe how you stood up for me with those skanks at the school that day, and you being the new girl. Man, you sure had them mesmerized when you threatened to call your sister's fiancé, a Major with the FLPD, and blab about the bullshit bullying that goes on in that dump and how the authorities turn a blind eye. You even made Vice Principle Miller back off and take our side. It was sweet. No one's ever done that for me before."

Charli made a grimace about the reference to her so-called fiancé but stayed glued to the conversation, a glow of pride igniting about Kayla taking a stand. The more time she spent with the teen, the more she became invested. The steel-enforced heart she only allowed air when she was with her gramps, had begun to beat in rhythm when she was with her protégé. Not sure how she felt about that, she stopped worrying and tuned in as the girls began talking again.

"Shitters, Angie, you looked so... oh crap, I don't know, mean, scared, like you didn't care what they did to you, but mostly, you looked... a-alone. You know? It really sucked."

"Yeah."

"That grabbed me. Maybe 'cause I've been there. I know your life's harsh right now, Angie, but you can make it better. Listen, an honest old lady once told me this a while back. Shocked the shit out of me, but her brutal words rang true. *No one gives a fuck about you. Everyone's too busy caring about their own shit. So, if you don't give a fuck either, you'll be lost, forgotten... end up a loser like so many others.*" Covers rustling made Charli think that one of the girls moved. "Don't you see? It's up to us to work hard, make something of ourselves and escape these crap lives we're in right now."

"Crap lives? You're talking crazy, dude. You have a sister you love, you live in a palace. Hold it! I'm not being a bitch, it's true. You have Charli and Blake on your side. Any blind fool can see they care about you. You're lucky. No one... and I mean no one... gives a flying fuck about me."

"I do." The sob in Kayla's voice came through, adding a compassionate resonance that rang with sincerity. "I care," she said in a soft, loving tone as if she needed the other girl to hear, to believe... to care, too.

"Oh God, Kayla. I prayed for help. Don't ever tell anyone I said this, but I can't take this shit any longer. I cut myself over and over, praying *He'd* see me and do something."

"I saw those marks on your thighs, Angie. They're horrible. Stop it. They won't help. Maybe God sent me to be your friend, to help you escape."

"Escape? Are you fucking kidding me? That fat slob will never let me go. Besides, I have an issue that's stopped me from running so many times.

You want to hear something really pathetic? I'm terrified of the dark. I mean, I can't breathe petrified. Last month, I did run and lasted three hours on the streets before I crawled back to the hellhole and got the shit beat outta me for getting home so late. I knew then, I was stuck. And things have gone way past the point where I can survive."

"You've got to. We'll make a plan. Charli will help you. I know she will. Just give it a bit more time."

"I can't. It's so painful. What that bastard does when he comes to my room. I've tried to fight him off but he's so much stronger. And the sick pervert forces me to do things I can't even tell you about. I hate him, and I hate her for not stopping him. God, I'm so full of hate that I hate myself most of all. Oh, Kayla, I'm sorry. Look, stop crying. I'll shut the fuck up. Stop it. You're breaking my heart."

Charli held her hand over her mouth and ran to the bathroom. Tears streaming, her heart in a mad mess from hearing those heartbreaking words, she barely made it behind the closed door before the reaction to Angie's allegations took over.

Oh my God!

Sickened beyond her ability to cope, she let loose – cried, hurled and bashed her fist against the sink in disgust. It took some time before she could blow her nose and shed the soft-hearted feelings of compassion. Eventually, her tough FBI code of ethics took over. Then and there, she made herself, and Angie, a promise.

Vile pricks like that bastard needed payback.

And she was just the girl to do it.

She couldn't wait.

Chapter Twenty-thre e

The next morning, after a nice breakfast that Kayla and Angie lightheartedly prepared, Charli purposely forced the issue to drive Angie home. Angie's attitude toward Charli had thawed slightly since the day before, but her dead-eyed look would still freeze-frame a more tender, kindly soul.

"I don't need a ride. I can walk. I want to walk."

"Tough. I intend to drive you home, kid, and that's that."

As they approached Angie's home and pulled to the ditch in front, Charli gave Kayla the warning look they both recognized. "I'm going in with Angie. Lock the car doors. And in case you feel the need, I left something for you in the glove box." This statement made no sense to Angie, but Kayla's expression took on a serious edge, and she nodded. Message received. She had protection.

Though both of the girls had stiffened with surprise, Kayla, used to taking orders from Charli, said nothing. Whereas, Angie tried to talk and got cut off. She finally shrugged and gave in.

"This won't take long." For the first time ever, Charli intended to leave Kayla in the car, but it couldn't be helped. She'd be safer here. Meanwhile, she escorted Angie to her door.

As they walked up the cracked sidewalk together, Charli saw the disrepair of the older home, the missing lawn replaced by weeds, rocks and dirt. The stringy sheet half-hanging in the dirty window, the broken-down steps leading to the door, adding to the appearance of a place no one cared about. Moving forward, she made sure that Angie stayed behind her.

As they reached the front door, she warned the startled girl, her voice firm, hard, no compromise at all. "You do exactly what I tell you, kiddo. Exactly. Got it?"

Stunned, Angie stared at her, a worried, scared look appearing. "Yeah, sure. What's up, Charli?"

"Let's go inside and you stay behind me, you hear?"

"But... like, what's wrong?" Angie clutched at her arm, stopping their forward momentum.

Charli's harsh tone belied her comforting words. "Just do as I say, right? We just have to get through these next few minutes, and I need you to be brave.

I've no doubt of the outcome, but in case things go to hell, you run back to the car, lock yourselves in and get Kayla to call 9-1-1. Got it?"

Totally bewildered, Angie nodded. The frightened look on her face showed that she'd picked up on Charli's seriousness but didn't know what brought about the change.

"Did I do something?"

"Shit, no." Charli reached out to touch the flinching girl's face. A gentle caress on the cheek was all she attempted and all she was allowed. "Okay, let's get this over with."

Charli took Angie's key from her hand and used it to open the door, then she walked into the house. The first thing she saw was a braless woman lying on the sofa, her grubby T-shirt barely covering her nakedness and her dirty white shorts missing a button. Straggly, unwashed hair and sores on her face, the woman's one eye drooped while the other gave an impression there was no one home.

"Angie? Honey? Is that you? Could you make me some toast? I haven't eaten anything since yesterday. Girl, are you listening?"

Charli waved Angie back and spoke up, "Mrs. Taylor? Angie's leaving. She'll be moving in with me for a while. Here's my card, the address is on the back. If you have any problems with this arrangement, call Major Blake Sebastian of the FLPD. He'll deal with any questions you have."

Charli gave Angie a tiny shove. "Go to your room and gather everything you need. I'll wait, honey. Don't worry. Go now."

Charli saw the tears explode out of the worried, enlarged eyes of the youngster. "Hank won't like it."

Mrs. Taylor piped up, her hysteria obvious. "You can't do this. She's my baby. My husband will stop you, see if he don't."

"I'd like to speak to your husband. Where is he?"

"No, Charli, don't. He'll hurt you."

"Like he hurts you? Not anymore. Never again. Go and do as I told you." She gently pushed the girl toward the stairs.

It was hard talking over the screeching racket erupting from the beauty queen who'd roused herself from the couch but didn't have the stamina to stand. Falling back, she forced herself forward again and was finally able to stumble toward the room off the kitchen, bellowing, "Hank, you get out here. There's a woman here, taking our Angie."

The door opened and the creepiest guy Charli'd seen in a long time shuffled out, half asleep. His overweight body looked like a walking boulder of muscle and flab, with short, skinny legs as props. Seeing a working man, one whose back and arms were most likely his tools of employment, and his belly a dumping ground for too much beer, she waited.

Eyes too close in the oversized head, hair missing

on top and puffed out like a wreath around the bottom part of his head, it hung long enough to hang over his thick neck. Weaving towards them, he pushed his stained white muscle shirt, the type the kids refer to as a wife-beater, into his droopy sweats and glowered. "Where's that bitch, Angie? Why'd you let her go away last night?"

"I never let her, idiot. She jis' took it on herself to stay away. You gotta talk to her, make her mind."

Suddenly, Hank looked over and saw Charli. His eyes narrowed when he saw the disgust she didn't attempt to hide. Not too stupid, he stomped to within a foot of her and sneered, "Get out of my house, cop."

"I'm no cop."

"Ya look like one to me, even smell like one. Whoever you are, fuck off."

"Make me."

"What'd you say?"

"Are you deaf as well as ugly? I said, make me."

Angie's moan broke the dead silence. Charli spoke as an offside, "Go pack, kiddo. You're coming home with me."

"What the fuck?"

"That's what I was tryin' to tell you, Hank. This cop... ahh, lady wants to take away our little Angel."

Hank snickered, spewing a sound like a giggle, his voice too high for a body so big. "You can call her angel. I call her bitch, and she's not going nowhere." He pointed at Angie and reiterated, "You listen to me, runt. You're not leaving, and that's it."

Charli cut in, "You're wrong, Hank. And, if you try to stop us, you'll be sorry."

"Okay, I've had enough of this nonsense." He grabbed Charli's arm to force her to the door... his first mistake. His second was not staying down when she flipped him over her hip and jabbed him hard in the stomach, once and then again.

Roaring with rage, knocking over a chair and lamp in his hurry to get to his feet... to get to her... he reached to punch, missed when she ducked and swung again.

Whipping her agile body out of his way, Charli's elbow caught him on his collar bone and then she used her feet. Kicking him hard between the legs, she stopped his forward momentum. Then to seal the deal, she kicked him in the chin when he bent over to clutch the painful area.

His screams didn't faze her one little bit, nor did his wife's. Smiling, she walked over to the man, stuck her heel into his groin and scrunched down hard... really hard. This time his squeals outranked those of the now crazed woman who'd run to hide on her couch.

Bending down, Charli added another dose of pressure and spoke, "You ever come near Angie again, you nasty prick, and I'll shoot you dead. That's after I aim for these naughty little boys, you understand me, Numb-nuts? You're a creepy sicko who should be in jail. And since my fiancé happens to be Major Blake Sebastian of the FLPD, I'll make sure and tell him about this little visit and why. Him and his boys, well they'd take great pleasure in making life a living hell for you from now on. So, listen to my warning and take me seriously. Leave – Angie – alone."

His pitiful moans still didn't faze her. In fact, she relished his cries. "And... one more thing. If I can talk Angie into filing charges against you, you'll be tried for rape. I'll make sure you get thrown into regular housing in maximum security where the boys hate men like you. They like to give them a taste of their own medicine, if you know what I mean."

Her words broke through the pain. He growled obscenities and pleas for help at the same time. "Fucking bitch, she's lying. I never touched her. God help me, I need an ambulance. I'm dying. Look what you done to me. I'm bleeding."

"Good."

"Fucking bitches. Go. See if I care. Get out." He pointed a shaking, dirty finger at Angie, who'd stayed frozen on the stairs. "Don't come back crying for forgiveness. Help me, Lora. Goddamn." Crying now, the pitiful animal blathered through his slobbering spit and runny nose.

Charli turned to see the girl frozen in place; a shocked look replacing the hard countenance she'd saved for Charli. Slowly, after Charli nodded yes, it's truly happening, shining through her tears, hope appeared – hope and joy.

Charli winked and grinned. "Unless, there's something here you particularly want, Angie, fuck the shit. I'll buy you whatever you need."

"There's just one item I can't leave. Will you wait? I'll be right back." Angie began racing up the rickety stairs but skidded to a stop. She fell backwards. Agile, driven by ramped up adrenalin; she righted herself in a split second. "Don't leave."

"I'll wait. Get whatever you want." Charli stood guard at the stairs and ignored the others.

Hurrying again, Angie reappeared a few seconds later clutching a visibly well-used teddy bear. "I couldn't leave him."

"No problem."

"He's my best friend."

Chapter
Twenty-four

The two walked out of the house, and on the porch, Charli felt a hand slip into hers, a smaller, softer, shaking hand. "Thank you." She heard the tears and stopped to turn, to hug. She withdrew a tissue from her pocket and wiped the girl's face.

"You are so welcome, little girl. You're mine now, and I'll never let anything bad happen to you again, you got that? Never. From now on you and me, we're a team."

"And Kayla?"

"Of course."

Kayla!

Charli started toward the car, and her heart stopped. The vehicle sat empty. Kayla was gone. *Shit, shit...* To be sure, she ran forward and searched inside.

Oh no! Fuck!

Suddenly, when she thought her legs would give

out, when the stress she'd controlled during the battle started to creep out of hiding and take over, she heard Angie say, "Kayla, where were you?"

Kayla?

Charli turned and took a long overdue breath. Suddenly angry, a reaction to her fear, she stomped over to Kayla and demanded, "Yeah. Where were you? I specifically warned you to stay in the car, and when I give you an order, girl, you follow it." Harsh words spit out in a voice that meant them, she hovered over the two younger girls now hugging.

Kayla didn't cower or appear intimidated. "Like you'd stay in the car if you heard the screams I heard. I had your weapon, not you. How did I know it wasn't you screaming? How could I stay safe if you needed me?"

Hearing the truth ringing throughout Kayla's words, she backed off and nodded, understanding that the girl had broken orders thinking to protect her. How in the hell could she stay mad at Kayla for doing exactly what she would have done in the same situation?

Before she could apologize, an approaching siren broke the silence, and she questioned Kayla with her stunned glare. "You didn't..."

"I had to. I thought it was you screaming in pain or maybe Angie. It sounded like a war zone. What would you have had me do? Twiddle my thumbs, ho-hum, and ignore everything? Get real."

"Yeah, okay. But I'm calling him off, and then we need to go home and set some new rules."

"Fine."

"Fine."

As they battled, Angie's head bobbed from Kayla to Charli and back again. Astonished glee that hadn't faded, transformed her back to a fourteen-year-old for the first time. Hugging her teddy bear added to that impression.

Kayla stepped to meet Blake, who'd arrived just as she knew he would... since it was his number she'd called. The weight of the weapon, hanging from her hand, reminded her she still clutched it. She shoved it toward Charli who quickly hid it in the back waistband of her dark pants.

The SUV skidded to a stop in the middle of the road, gravel flying, and Blake erupted like he'd been shot from a cannon. "What's up, Kayla?" As soon as he saw the three girls safe and together, his demeanor changed from a rescuing cop under a great deal of pressure to a man unsure of his welcome. "You sounded terrified, said Charli was in trouble." Charli saw his eyes moving, taking in everything at once, the way he'd been trained.

"Yeah, I panicked. Charli and Angie are fine. Right?" She turned to face the other two.

Both nodded, and to be sure, Charli spoke to her new responsibility. "You okay, kiddo?"

Angie's beatific smile broke out, belying the tear-streaked face. "I'm perfect." No sooner had those words left her lips than she broke. This time her wails wouldn't be hushed until Kayla wrapped her arms around her and led her to their car. "It's okay, Angie. Whatever happened, everything will be fine."

Angie started babbling like a tap with a broken valve. "You should have seen her. Charli flipped that big bastard, Hank, on his ass and then kicked him in the balls, had him crying like a baby. It was the most beautiful thing I ever saw. He never knew what hit him." Angie's loud voice, overflowing with excitement, shock and tremendous joy, ensured that Blake heard her every word.

All the time the girl rambled on; he stared at Charli until his arms swept her into a bear hug she couldn't break loose.

"What are you...? Stop it." She struggled but he wouldn't let her go.

"Were you hurt? You're shaking. I can feel it."

"It's just a shitty stress thing I'm dealing with," she hissed in his ear. "The girls are watching. Seriously, back off or I won't be responsible for what'll happen."

Being nobody's fool, he stepped back and held up his hands.

"Calm down sweetheart. Right now, they're smiling, so don't spoil the moment. By the way, Angie is crying happy tears, I can tell. And Kayla's squeals are filled with pure joy. You need to share. I can use some good news too."

Blake turned to Charli who now leaned against the rented car, her arms wrapped around herself, her legs weak at the thought of the responsibility she'd just taken on. She'd been so obsessed in her need to get Angie revenge; she'd forgotten a few rather important details.

She was in a witness protection program with a fourteen-year-old girl, hiding in fear for her life.

And she'd just committed herself to another fourteen-year-old... this time forever.

Jesus help me, what the hell was I thinking?

Chapter
Twenty-five

John Madison hadn't really been serious about his plans to go to Fort Lauderdale, not really. But finding a dead body in his apartment had totally revised his thinking – big time.

He hadn't known that Mark Crawly planned a visit with him that day, not until he found the detective beaten around the face and dead in his easy-boy chair; the one Charli had insisted he needed because the electric mechanism lifted him for easier standing.

The problem he had with the sucker was when he'd fall asleep and his arm accidently pressed the up-button, he'd wake up just as his body flew through the air to land a few feet across the room. He'd blessed the position of his sofa across from the chair, giving him a soft landing more times than he'd admit.

Stop it! He wiped his eyes and blew his nose.

Hands shaking terribly, he rubbed them against his knees, reenacting familiar behavior before the pain-relieving days of yoga exercises for the elderly, a knee replacement, and best of all, his B.C. Bud Rub.

Stop rambling, old man, and ignoring the inevitable. Reviewing the horrific scene, his sluggish brain had trouble taking it in. Like a spoiled puppy, most of his days were spent eating and sleeping with the occasional fun activity thrown in. The only occasions where he cared enough to stay alert were spent with his FBI granddaughter.

It's time to deal with reality, John-boy. You can't escape what's right in front of you.

Mark hadn't had the luxury of escape either. It appeared that the old cop had taken quite a thrashing before he'd been put out of his misery. Was this done by the same killer he'd read about? Oh God, had the killer executed Mark, trying to get answers to Charli's whereabouts – tortured him until he talked?

Not that Mark could have given away all that much. Once, after too much wine and John's constant sly probing, he'd shaken his head bemused by John's unwillingness to give up. "I'm not taking any chances on your girl's safety, John. Not that I know a lot about her whereabouts now that she's in the system anyway. But she's a good agent, and you should be proud of her for stepping up and doing her duty."

John computed Mark's "in the system" comments, her taking on a special job and everything else he'd managed to piece together, with her being in witness protection. He presumed, either someone else could ID the murderer they'd written about in the paper, or she was the witness herself.

Either way, she'd gone into hiding. And he'd bet the farm that the killer had done his best to find out where. But an old soldier like Mark wouldn't have spilled the beans. Would he?

Suddenly, a sledge hammer of understanding hit him hard, and had him falling back against the sofa that had provided him a soft landing so many times before.

That murdering bastard came here to question me!

That makes the most sense. He thought I knew something, found Mark waiting for me in my chair and probably mistook us.

Okay, this could only mean one thing. Sure as shit, the killer was after his Charli.

Wake up, old fool. Grab a few things and get your rickety old ass out of here. It's too late to save Mark, but you need to disappear before they stop you from trying to warn her.

Circling the apartment like a chicken with his head cut off, John grabbed an old tote bag, some underwear, shirts, pants and socks and then stopped.

Scratching his head, needing to think straight,

he waited. When new thoughts bombarded, he took off again. This time, he snagged his passport, iPad, phone, wallet and all the cash he'd stuffed in hiding places around the joint.

Suddenly, he thought of his laptop and knew he didn't want the cops to find the latest searches he'd done when they worked the crime scene. With it under his arm, he headed to Brad's apartment.

Banging loudly, knowing the old fart had probably fallen asleep after supper, he walked in and sure enough, there he sat, snoring away in his chair.

He thought for a minute and tiptoed forward. Actually, this worked even better. Rather than asking Brad to hide the computer, and then lying to the questions he'd no doubt have to answer, he'd just tuck it away somewhere his old friend wouldn't notice it.

Sneaking into the man's bedroom, blessing God for giving him strong limbs so he needed no walker or walking aids other than the occasional cane on rainy days, he opened the closet to hide his laptop.

Just as he went to close the door, he spotted a thin leather binder with the word "Documents" embossed in gold lettering. Quickly, he opened it and amongst the papers, he found Brad's passport and his old medical card. Grabbing both, plus the unopened bottle of extra strength Tylenol his pal ate like candy, he let himself out without rousing his friend.

First checking to see if the corridor was clear, he hurried back to his place to collect his gear. Needing to scat before someone came into his apartment and tried to stop him, he headed for the back door, fingered in the security code to unlock it and headed to the nearest restaurant.

There he approached a young lady, asked if she'd be so kind as to use her phone to call him a taxi, and was tickled when after inquiring where he wanted to go, she offered him a ride.

Small town, good-hearted folks... God love 'em.

***

Hours later and many towns away from home, John had his new friend drop him off at an airport hotel where he settled down to catch a flight first thing in the morning. He didn't care where it flew, as long as they didn't look too closely at the photo in his new passport.

He knew for a fact that most officials never really scrutinized old people. It had been happening a lot over these last few years, him passing under the radar like he had no importance to the world.

He figured it meant they hated any reminders of their own approaching futures. If he wore the glasses he'd bought at a convenience store, combed all his hair back from his forehead and pretended to be a grouch, surely they'd see Brad.

Wrestling his eyes open yet again, waiting for his wake-up call, his mind wandered to Charli. If she'd followed through with her plans to go to Fort

Lauderdale, and he located the house she'd rented, just maybe he'd find her there, warn her... protect her.

If unsuccessful, it wouldn't be for the lack of trying. The idea of failure brought back the heart palpitations he'd been fighting off ever since he found Mark. He took another sip of his tea. *Face it, man. You need to get lost for a while, and what better place?*

Not being too stupid, he knew the killer had somehow linked him to Charli, and that wasn't good. He couldn't be used to trap his girl. Hell, she'd do anything; even give herself to a killer to save her old popsicle.

Damned if he'd let that happen. The only relief he got from Mark's death was praying that the killer believed Mark to be him.

***

Late the next day, after sleeping on the various flights and getting wheelchair assistance in the airports, he arrived in Fort Lauderdale. Though the heat sucked the little energy he had left, pure gumption, or what Charli alluded to as his mule-headedness, kept him going. With the help of an accommodating taxi driver, he found a nice hotel, freaked at the outrageous cost for the two nights but forked it over, and rented a boat with a driver to tour the waterways the next morning.

He grinned ruefully and shrugged at the same time. Penny-pinching no longer mattered. He needed to find his girl.

Chapter
Twenty-six

Earlier, Blake's heart pounding, pitching battles inside his chest, he'd floored it to the address that Kayla had shared, the siren screaming all the way. He'd broken every road rule and had arrived even before the back-up.

Once he'd seen the three girls standing outside the dump-like house, and they appeared fine, the dryness in his mouth became flooded with an abundance of saliva. For a few seconds, he thought he'd lose his lunch.

Charli stood beside the other two; ramrod straight, her soft blonde curls haloing her head. Tight black pants sculpted her perfect ass, her long legs tucked inside fitted black boots. Paired with a snug white shirt, a cover emphasizing perky breasts he'd dreamed of too often lately, he unclenched the wheel.

Damn, that woman has me wound so tight, I can't

think straight.

Leaving his vehicle in the middle of the road, he'd quickly approached Kayla who stepped forward, her eyes warning even while her lips explained.

Listening, he searched the area, and when he felt he'd hidden his angst enough to approach a now cranky Charli, Angie's words had painted a picture he'd have given his next paycheck to have seen. Charli laying a beating on a deserving fat asshole and winning, well... how straight-up fucking awesome.

He relished the word-picture, until he looked at Charli's face and saw the reaction to Angie's words.

Hugging her hadn't been planned, just an instinct he couldn't fight. He didn't know anyone who needed his arms around them more than the shaking mess in front of him. Aha! She wasn't Superwoman after all. The fight had taken its toll.

Nope.

While he'd forced her close, her whispered warning stirred his memory.

Stress! The report he'd poured over yet again the night before came back with a vengeance. The Bureau's psychologist strongly advised that Charli be given a period of timeout – meaning personal leave to get her head straight.

In dire need to recoup from an earlier extended case, one where she'd handled crushing tension, constant peril, and in the end, a battle where many died, the doctor hadn't minimized his diagnosis. Charli needed to rest, take a vacation. No working for the foreseeable future. And... under no circumstances, have any undue stress in her life.

***

Hours later, Blake appeared at their dinner table and made his announcement. "I'll be moving back home tonight."

Angie and Kayla grinned and voiced their support. "Sweet!"

Charli reacted somewhat differently. Her chair skidded before it flipped over. Her face lost its color, and her voice rose just slightly lower than a full-out scream.

"What?"

Inside he flinched but forced an outer calm. Taking on the boss-like tone he used to run a police department full of hot-heads, he added, "There's no argument you can say to make me change my mind, I'll be around a lot more, so suck it up, sweetheart."

Chapter Twenty-seve n

Earlier, calming from her panic to where she could see a doable future with Angie, it took Charli a while to lay down new rules for both her wards. The need to wiggle around Angie's questions, obliged to play it safe; she purposefully didn't reveal a lot of information.

The pitiful few questions Angie did ask surprised her. As if the girl still existed in a dream she didn't want to wake up from, she became agreeable to whatever Charli said. In fact, she couldn't have been more affable. Knowing that would change soon enough, the relief Charli felt at the moment was huge. Since she didn't have answers, not having questions right now worked for her.

Shaking, not able to relax after the earlier battle

with scumbag Hank, she overcame her reluctance and used one of the pills her doctor had prescribed for such moments. They were awful, made her sluggish and off-center, like she was drunk. She'd have benefited a whole lot more from an hour of yoga or hard physical exercise. Unfortunately, she had no time.

First, she'd talked privately with Kayla, where after an intense argument that Charli had trouble following, the highly intelligent teen agreed that it wouldn't be fair for Angie to stay with them – to possibly put her life at risk.

Even though the danger level had minimized with each passing day nothing happened with Dylan Ross, it would be wrong to take any chances, nor would the department approve.

Therefore, the next day, Charli would look into a private school in Seattle, close to the smaller town where her grandfather lived, and request that Mark Crawly look after the details. She'd also ask him to instigate a meeting between John Madison and Angie and share her wishes with John that he should take the young girl under his wing until Charli returned.

Once they had Dylan in custody, she'd let Angie decide her future, hers – and if she could wrangle through the red tape, Kayla's. Let them choose a school where they could be together, and she'd pay. Hell, what better way to spend some of her inheritance than to give two deserving girls a chance in life. A way they could stay together if they so wished.

Everything had settled down to where she felt better, more relaxed, could breathe without the constriction around her chest tightening uncomfortably. She'd been cool, even looked forward to Blake arriving that evening for dinner.

That he'd been late didn't faze her. That he'd dumped a bombshell in the middle of their Scrabble game, well... that did it!

"I'll be moving back home tonight."

Angie and Kayla grinned, high-fived and voiced their support. "Sweet."

Charli reacted somewhat differently. Her chair skidded before it flipped over. Her face lost its color, and her voice rose just slightly lower than a full-out scream.

"What?"

He flinched even while he took on the boss-like tone he likely used to run a police department full of hot-heads. "There's no argument you can say to make me change my mind. I'll be around a lot more, so suck it up, sweetheart."

She was pissed.

Glaring his way, she gritted her order between teeth that she'd forced closed to keep in the vitriol she couldn't flay him with in front of witnesses. "In the bedroom. We need to talk." She stomped down the hallway and heard the nervous giggles the girls shared at whatever stupidly cute comment he'd no doubt shared.

As soon as he closed the door, she whipped around, hands on hips, and let it rip. "There's no blasted way in hell you're moving in here while I'm under this roof. Either things stay the way they are, or we leave."

Obviously working to keep his cool, Blake glared back, and then he said words she couldn't argue with, words that stopped her cold.

"He killed her. Agent Melissa Dale, the one who took your place at the house you rented, he tortured her first. And then he killed her."

Charli sagged, about to drop, and Blake gathered her close. "I'm sorry for giving you the news so brutally. But I need you to understand why I'm adamant about you and the girls having sufficient protection until we can move you out."

"Of course. Oh my God. I'm so sorry. I never thought he'd find out about my personal plans for renting that house." Charli's head swam in a morass of guilt and pain for the other agent and her family. "That bastard's not going to stop, is he?"

"Nope. We never thought he would. He wants Alicia Shoal and killing anyone in his way won't even register on his guilt-meter. In fact, the monster doesn't have one."

"I know. You're right. Thank God we've changed our identities and Agent Dale didn't know where we were heading."

Blake turned away but not in time. She saw his

face.

"What? You're not telling me something."

"He broke into your apartment."

"In Seattle? When?"

"Two days ago."

"Hold it. When did he kill Agent Dale?"

"After the police finish their investigation, we'll know more. But from the crime scene, and the neighbors who were with her in the early part of the evening, I'd say last night."

"So, he was in town this morning. And I left Kayla in a car by herself."

"With a loaded gun. You were slightly busy beating the shit out of Angie's dad. Who, by the way, ended up in the hospital with some pretty bad damage to his precious boys. He's claiming it was an accident." At her probing look, he added, "We get notified whenever anyone appears in the emergency room with questionable injuries. I paid him a little visit before I got the news about Agent Dale's murder. He won't be bothering you or Angie ever again. And he promised he'd turn over any documents she'd have need of, and he'd get his wife to sign away any rights on papers that the court draws up." Blake closed the gap between them and gently tugged her into his arms, hugging her close.

Charli's arms clung around his waist and her head rested on his wide shoulders. Feeling protected, like she did as a little girl perched on her daddy's knee, she let the tears fall. Tears that wouldn't be held in any longer.

"That poor woman."

"She put up a fight, Charli, but in the end, I figure she gave him whatever information she had."

"Which was nothing, right?"

"Which was that you and Alicia were in Fort Lauderdale."

"Seriously? Shit."

"Seriously."

"That's a game changer, isn't it?"

"Oh, yeah. He's closer than I ever thought he'd get."

"What do we do now? Should we move?"

"As soon as we can get arrangements made, yes. Until then, I have a full detail posted around the house. For now, we'll hunker down here until either we get the all-clear that they have the son of a bitch in custody, or they've arranged a new safe house."

His hands gathered her face, and he stared into her soft brown eyes, shining with unshed tears. Sorrow, visible in their gorgeous depths, made them gentler than he'd ever seen them before.

Kissing her mouth, a simple touch of sympathy, he hugged her even tighter. "I need to keep you safe."

"Me and Kayla, and now Angie. Poor girl's caught up in this too."

"I know. If you feel its best, we could take her to a safe house where she'd be looked after."

Snuggling closer, ignoring warnings blaring from her brain that she was allowing him a lot more leeway than she usually let any man, Charli admitted, "Already made a similar suggestion. Her answer was a simple – no way in hell. That girl can become an iceberg when she's not happy."

"No doubt she's spent most of her life in that condition. I saw her old man."

"Yeah. If I don't keep her with me now, she'll be lost... her chance wasted. She needs affirmation that she matters, that someone cares. Earlier, when we were at her house, she had it. I gave it to her. We can't take the chance that she'll misinterpret the reason she shouldn't stay now. The damage could be irreparable. That kid's on the brink of doing something stupid. She's that close to taking her own life."

"God, Charli. She's a good kid. See how she's taken to Kayla, how the two of them are together?"

"I know. I've watched them, saw them sharing these last few hours, and it's beautiful." Charli told him what she'd overheard the night before. How even in her depths of despair, Angie thought to reach out to others by donating her hair and organs. And how her young body had been tortured repeatedly by an animal who didn't give a rat's ass about the harm or pain he caused. To his credit, Blake listened without interrupting.

After she'd finished, he questioned her, his husky tones filled with understanding. "So, you decided the Neanderthal needed a lesson, and she needed to see it. You did what I would have done in your place. The shit deserved everything he got and more. From now on, my people will be watching both her parents. They just have to step out of line, and I mean a tippy-toe over, and we'll book them with whatever we can. In the meantime, I see what a pickle you're in with Angie."

"Yep. I'm taken with the girl, her guts and deep-down sweetness. Not sure how it happened, but both her and Kayla have snuck into... ahh, mattering. Now I need to keep them safe."

Without releasing her, he arched back so he could see her eyes when asking his question. "So, you're good about me staying?"

She tried pulling away but gave up the struggle when she sensed he needed her to stay, to answer... to relieve his worry. "I guess, as long as we make some rules – keep things between us impersonal. No more hugs and kissing. Just two cops on a job."

"Bullshit, Charli. You know I can't keep my hands off you. You're like a magnet for me. There's nothing impersonal about what I feel when I'm around you."

Her voice steely, Charli reacted, "Buddy, it's called lust. So quit acting like I'm a bitch in heat and back off." She pushed away from him and stopped a foot away.

Hoping she'd get him so pissed he'd leave her alone, she made her expression reflect her hard words. God, she needed him to stop torturing her with his smell, his strength... his nearness. The last thing she wanted in her crazy, mixed-up life was a horny man who had somehow broken through her barriers left open from two teens she couldn't resist.

His reaction shocked her. First he grinned, making her nervous, his handsome face adoringly more so with the soft light in his mystical green eyes. And then he made his move. Within seconds, he'd hoisted her into his arms, his lips demanding.

Any options left open completely faded, she lifted her arms around his neck, and her legs around his waist.

Like she weighed less than a child, he boosted her, and then used the nearest wall for support. Without hesitation, his expert kisses forced her response. His tongue delved into her mouth and made love to her, pushing in and out until every bone in her body melted from unleashed passion.

Any thoughts of stopping him fled as she immersed herself in the torrid swells of erotic emotion. Incited, on fire, she changed from breathing normally to panting, and knew he suffered the same condition. That knowledge aroused her even more.

His hands undid her bra and began forcing it and her top over her head, and she willingly held up her arms to make it easier. On their downward move, his hands cradled her butt to put her body in perfect position with his own thickness.

Meanwhile, her hands caressed his head, sliding through his hair, cradling his cheeks, holding him in place. He'd gotten her attention, her involvement. Now, there'd be no stopping. She needed him, needed his hardness inside her... to feel alive again. She'd lived in a vacuum without sex for far too long.

"You're so beautiful, baby. I love your hair." After gliding up over her bare back and shoulders, his hands were now entangled in her curls. Twinges of pain from him tugging the strands added to her hunger. God, how she wanted to feel attached to another soul in the way humans were meant to be – their bodies joined.

Their hearts beating hard in unison.

Their breaths gasping together in ecstasy.

"Hmmm." She wouldn't answer, couldn't. He had her attention, held her captive. No way would she give him bits of her heart through her voice.

Each time they moved, their body's grinding into each other's, back and forth, from side to side, she mashed her chest to his. Taking the hint, Blake cupped her loosened breasts as they swayed and bounced.

Lowering his head, he bathed them with his tongue. "You're gorgeous, your body is perfect." His kisses travelled until he stopped at her nipples.

"These babies are so pretty. God, Charli, you're so sweet. So sweet."

Allowing him full access, she wrapped her arms around his lowered shoulders and soaked in the sensuous reactions. Her body throbbed, her groin tingled, dampened, waiting, writhing, the palpitations overwhelming. She wanted him inside her.

His whispered pleas revealed a similar reaction. "I need you, baby. Like it's crazy. I need you so bad."

His lips returned to hers. He kissed her like she'd never been kissed before, searching, overcoming, demanding a response she'd refused to share until now. Heart beat thudding, her legs went weak...

And then the house alarm screamed.

Chapter Twenty-eigh t

That's the house. John knew it. Just as he knew he'd better be careful approaching. Charli might mistake him for a bad guy. He grinned at the foolishness of his thought.

Hold it! What if his whole premise had been wrong and Charli wasn't even there. Best he find out before he went messing around and some stranger didn't like his questions.

Once he paid the boat driver, he'd take a taxi one street over and wait until it got dark. But first, he'd buy some of those binoculars like the ones he had at home; small, powerful ones like those he used when they went to the theatre.

If he could approach from the beach without anyone seeing him, he might be able to zoom into a window and recognize his girl before ringing the doorbell.

If she didn't show, he'd bring flowers the next day and pretend he was a delivery man. Hell, he'd seen enough cop shows to know that worked for them.

Later that night, following his plan, he found himself on the beach not far from the property he'd located. Crouching, which wasn't easy at his age, he managed to work his way around the property until he'd positioned himself behind a flowering bush that hid him well.

The overpowering scent kept his mind occupied and had him searching his memory for the name of the beautiful orchid-like pink flower. Busy, he didn't notice the man who'd stopped at a vehicle on the street until he approached the house and let himself in with some kind of burglary tools.

Shit! What the hell had he gotten himself into? Breathing heavily, he rose to warn his baby but stopped when he saw the woman who'd fallen asleep on the sofa rise.

Chapter
Twenty-nine

Blake started from the room first and Charli grabbed a sweater she could zip up and her weapon before following. She heard him giving orders to the girls.

"Turn those lights off and get into the pantry. Lock the door, both locks." Blake's orders made sense. She'd noticed the security cameras in that room after he'd warned her he'd recently made it a kind of safe room, a place for them to go if they had any unexpected visitors.

Before she headed to search the rest of the house, she made sure the teens did as they were told. Now behind Blake, who'd retrieved a weapon from some hidey-hole she knew nothing about, they started to split up. His hand signals, sending her in the opposite direction, consigned him to be the boss. Fine with her! She didn't have to deal alone so whatever he wanted, she'd be his partner.

When the doorbell rang, they stopped dead, both stunned. *What the hell?* First time she'd heard of an intruder with killing on his mind demand entrance by ringing the doorbell.

The voice of one of his men pounding on the door and yelling louder than the ear-splitting alarm made Blake stand down. With her at his back, her gun behind her, ready to shoot if the circumstances warranted, he turned off the system, released the locks and opened the door – a few inches at first, then wider.

Charli saw the uniform, and the mortified face of Blake's officer who'd set off the alarm.

"Dudley? Jesus, man, are you trying to give us a heart attack in here? You should have phoned before approaching within a foot of the house. I warned you guys."

"I know, but this gentleman was in a hurry, and he slipped past us before I could stop him. Seems he saw the murder of Agent Dale and would only talk to you in person." The man in question stepped into the light.

"Popsicle!"

Charli stepped out from behind Blake.

"Charli?"

Chapter
Thirty

John Madison couldn't believe his eyes when he saw his precious granddaughter move from behind the body of the big man who'd opened the door.

"Charli? Charli! Damn, girl, it's good to see you." He reached for her, his arms shaking with relief. Tears had gathered, and before he knew they would spill, his face became drenched, and his whole body shuddered from the reaction of seeing her in person. Something he'd thought might never happen.

After watching the murderer at work earlier, he'd given up hope of surviving himself. Unable to move for fear he'd be shot, he'd used the set of binoculars he'd bought that morning and witnessed the victim fighting for her life, and then being overwhelmed by the larger man with the gun.

For seconds, John thought she would win, but

the gun made the difference. While the animal worked her over as if he demanded answers to questions, John thought to get help. He used that moment to slide away but for some reason, he turned back just in time to see her being shot.

Dropping his binoculars, he half-ran, half-stumbled along as fast as his poor old body could handle in the direction of the neighbor's house up the beach.

Out of breath, he stopped, leaned against a post and reached into his pocket for the new cellphone he'd bought that morning. Son of a gun. He couldn't make it work. His old phone, he had no trouble with anymore, but this newfangled piece of shit, he couldn't even remember how to get to the phone section.

Grumbling, more angry and frustrated with his own shortcomings than usual, he made it to the closest house and pounded on their door, all to no avail. The place was locked – shut tighter than spinster Harriet's mouth was after seeing a half-naked man on the cover of a sport's magazine.

His breath coming in gasps, afraid of having a heart attack, considering his old pump thudded away in his chest with shooting pains to remind him of his age, he searched for a place to hide, to gather his strength... to think.

A pergola, nestled inside a garden of winding, colorful blooms, appeared out of the darkness, and he made his way there. With his legs finally giving out, John slid to the floor and rested. Sick to his stomach because of the overwhelming relief he'd felt that the young lady hadn't been his precious Charli, and angry for not having a weapon he could have used to protect her, he covered his face and let the tears flow.

Never, in all his years, had he felt quite so useless, so ashamed, and thankful all at the same time.

Chapter
Thirty-one

Blake and the girls had been super about allowing her and Popsicle a few minutes alone. They needed this time to reunite, to hug and explain. Charli had no idea how her grandfather had found her, and why he was even here in Fort Lauderdale.

On the other hand, she did know that Blake had to be bursting at the seams to interview him. She'd overheard his officer reporting that John Madison had witnessed Agent Dale's murder. Therefore, the old guy had a lot of explaining to do.

She knelt in front of him, making sure of his comfort in the easy chair she'd coaxed him into. "Calm down, Gramps." Her hands gently massaged his sore old knees while wishing she had some of his favorite Bud Rub cream to relieve the pain.

"He's dead, Charli. I liked him a lot and that murderous bastard killed him like he didn't matter at all."

What? He? All this stress is too much for him. He's losing it.

Not sure what the hell he rambled on about, Charli studied his expression, his still-wet eyes, and her heart ached for his misery. The only time she'd seen him looking his years and hurting this badly was after his wife had passed, and it had broken her heart.

She leaned in and hugged him again. Then she held his pale, whiskery cheeks in her hands and murmured, "Tell me everything, sweetheart."

"I keep seeing his battered face. He's dead, because of me."

Scared now, Charli hardened her tone. She needed to get to the bottom of his rambling. "I think you must be mixed up, Grandpa. He killed Agent Dale, Melissa Dale. She was a woman."

"Yeah, that too. You know kiddo; the devil's got a special place in hell for vermin like him." His eyes searched her face to make sure she'd heard his teachings, just like he used to do when she was a kid and he had a point to make that he wanted her to understand. His eyes would shoot fireballs that froze her, like they were right now.

"Got it, Grandpa." Totally messed up, not sure if it was her who'd made the mistake or the old darling had lost it completely, she stopped him. "Look, Gramps, I love you more than puppies or teddy bears, but you're not making any sense. Let me get you a cup of tea—"

"And some Tylenol if you have any and make it extra-strength."

Searching to see if her pill-hating grandpa was messing with her, and seeing his request as legitimate, she nodded. "Take a minute to clear your thoughts. I'll be right back."

She headed for the kitchen where the girls were huddled with Blake. "Do any of you have any Tylenol? Grandpa's breaking down old barriers and wants drugs. Never thought I'd see the day. He used to consider them the hard stuff compared to the occasional baby aspirin he'd allow himself."

Kayla spoke up. "I have some in my room. Is it safe to go and get them?"

"I'll come with you." Angie held out her hand, and acting like a bodyguard, she checked the hallway before allowing Kayla to leave the room. *Smart-ass kid!* Charli grinned and turned to see Blake grinning too.

Charli studied the man she'd recently been kissing and saw a guy with a handsome face, a gorgeous, muscular, lean body that turned women to mush and sexy green eyes that were now hooded. There was no time to find out why; her priorities had to be her family. "He needs a cup of tea, Blake. Can you make it strong and sweet? I think you need to hear what he has to say. He's making no sense to me."

Blake grabbed a mug from a stand of six, popped

a teabag inside and filled it with boiling water from the special tap he'd had installed at the sink. After adding the sugar, he placed some chocolate cookies he'd stashed away on a plate and followed Charli to where John waited.

John, slumped in the chair with his feet up on the footrest, had removed his shoes, and he lay there asleep. Charli hated to disturb him, but they needed to hear his story.

"Gramps, wake up. Here's some tea." He pried his eyes open and shook his head as if clearing away ugly hovering visions that popped into his conscious memory.

"Oh, Charli. It's a sad, sad world, baby. A sad world."

"I know, Gramps, but like you always told me, there's a half-full side in the glass, right? It helps. Like now. Look around, both of us are alive and safe."

John sat up in his chair, straightened his spine and let his eyes wander from her to the man who had crouched on the opposite side of his chair. A strange look came into his eyes, and he leaned back and smiled. "Yes. You're right, kiddo. There's still a half-full glass. Now, where's those hard drugs?"

As if she'd waited in the wings, Kayla appeared with the bottle of Tylenol, her inquisitive expression obvious. Rather than ask any questions, she took the hand John Madison extended in thanks and squeezed. Both their expressions lit up and Charli saw the man who had the gift make one more adoring fan.

Chapter Thirty-two

"Charli hasn't introduced us yet, but I'm Major Blake Sebastian with the Fort Lauderdale Police Department. I'm personally taking care of Charli and Kayla. Now, can you tell me what happened earlier, and why you suddenly appeared at the office downtown?"

Downtown? Charli swung Blake's way, an inquiry clear in her gaze. She still had no idea how her gramps had come to be here.

"My officer, Lieutenant Newton, just advised me that you'd arrived with information on a shooting you'd witnessed earlier, and that you would only talk to the man in charge." Blake spoke to John, looked in his direction, but she knew he was sharing with her at the same time.

"Yes. He's a good man. Tried to make me comfortable and told me he wasn't sure how long you'd be, that I could tell him what I'd seen. But, I wasn't about to blab out confidential information to just anyone. I watch enough TV to know it's best to deal with the top gun. He respected my wishes, said he'd try to contact you. So, I told him to hurry, that it was pretty obvious the woman was dead but they should send his people to make sure because miracles do happen, right?"

"I bet that got his attention," Blake grinned and John answered with one of his own.

"It did. He left, and your other youngster, Deputy Dudley, took over. No more nice guy now. He began drilling me like a hard rock miner."

Blake coughed, "You mean Detective Dudley Holler?"

"Okay. Whatever the idiot's name was, I don't remember. I do know one thing; he should go back and redo his officer's training. The man's a thug."

"Grandpa!"

Turning her way, he spoke with asperity, "You gotta call a spade a spade, kiddo. Just saying... the guy needs a punch in the nose to straighten out his attitude. Good thing I'm twice his age or I'da taken on that delightful chore myself."

"Settle down, now." Charli loved seeing the color return to her grandfather's face. It indicated that he still had some of his old grit. "What happened next?"

"Newton returned, and he became mighty serious. When he asked me my name, he got even more so. I figured someone must have verified the address, and that there was a body. That's when he agreed to bring me to you."

Charli wondered if it had more to do with his name being the same as hers. She knew hers and Kayla's records were closed, but surely, the top detective working under Blake would have been given certain details. This Bob Newton might have known her and John Madison could be related. And if he questioned him on his home address, that would have rung bells too.

Blake's next comment cut into her thoughts. "No doubt that's why he agreed to bring you here."

"I guess. My hinting at a heart problem that could kick up at any minute if I didn't get my way probably helped convince him too." John's smirk and wink at Charli had her chuckling.

What a naughty old brat! God, she loved him...

"What I didn't know was that he'd bring me to my girl." Reaching out to caress her cheek and ruffle her curls, John's hand trembled.

Charli took it and laid a kiss on his knuckles, not caring that her tender ministrations would be viewed by Blake. Now wasn't the time to rebuild her walls against that man, although they were forming by themselves as they always did after she'd lower them.

"Can you describe what you saw, sir? My men have verified Miss Dale's death, plus the death of two officers who were guarding her house. They were found in their vehicle, terminated by a pro."

"I didn't see them."

"That's the idea. They were there to protect Miss Dale."

"That's terrible. But they weren't no protection... nope. Maybe they needed to go back for more training, like Dudley."

"Grandpa!"

"Sorry, Charli. Just calling it as I—"

"Yes, we get it. Tell us what happened to you. How did you get close enough to the house to be a witness? And, why were you there in the first place? And who was the man you said was dead? Can you start from the beginning? This whole mess is making my head spin."

John handed her the bottle of Tylenol. "Take a couple of these suckers. They'll make the pain disappear faster than a—"

"Grandpa!"

"Okay, okay. I'm putting off having to tell you about Mark."

"Mark Crawly?" Blake looked lost. " I talked to him just a few days ago." His gaze lifted to Charli for answers.

Charli shrugged. Her eyes swiveled to the old man, and she said, "Tell us what happened, Gramps."

"Okay. So, Charli, after you left, Mark came to visit every few days, and we hit it off. He's a... *was* a good man. Just so you know, he never let on where you'd gone, but I figured it out from a show I used to watch that you maybe went into witness protection."

"Seriously? From an old TV show? How could you jump to that conclusion?"

"Because when you'd go on undercover jobs, you always managed to call every few days. This time, you warned me that wouldn't happen. And then, Mark dropped the ball just the one time after I convinced him to share with me—"

"You mean, you nagged him."

John waggled his head from one side to the other, "Yeah, okay, so I nagged for a little more information. What did you think? I could handle day after day with no word from you? Drove me batty."

"Which means, he let something out."

"What he said was – you were in the program. I couldn't get near you, it would be too dangerous, and I should just be proud that you were such a good agent."

Still not getting it, she asked, "So... from that you determined I must be in witness protection?"

"Not until me and Brad found the story about a shooting in the apartment across from yours. The one that happened the night before you told me you'd be going away."

Blake shook his head, confused and not hiding it. "Brad?"

"He's a friend of my grandpa's, lives at the same lodge."

John cut in, "And he used to be a big-shot reporter for the *Los Angeles Times*."

Charli sat back on her heels, stunned. "That old hypochondriac? I didn't know."

Before John could do anything but nod, Blake jumped in. "So, between the two of you researching crimes and coming up with a plausible answer, you figured out that Charli was in danger and had gone into witness protection. But how come you assumed she'd be coming to Fort Lauderdale?"

"'Cause I know my little girl. She's like her grandma, gets focused on one thing and woe betide anyone who tries to change her mind. She'd already planned her vacation and had chosen Fort Lauderdale for personal reasons. In fact, we were both supposed to come here, stay together and rekindle some sweet old memories. She'd even shown me the photo of the house she'd rented." John winked at her, his way of saying – pay attention.

"Aha! You wily old fox. That's how you did it. You've been here so many times, you recognized the neighborhood from the images they showed online." Charli stopped herself and then changed her mind. "Hold it. All you could see in those pictures was the outside angle of the house and the waterfront. How did you figure out which house when there's so many?"

"They had the sun setting behind them in the

photos and the one you'd rented had a stained glass window on the top bedroom floor. It was easy, Charli, come on."

Nodding after hearing his explanation, she grinned at Blake's confusion and added, "Now you know where I get my brilliant mind from – my gramps."

John turned to Blake, a huge smile lighting his proud face. "Ain't she cute?"

Charli cut them off. "She's a United States Special Agent for the Federal Bureau of Investigation. That's what she is." Her harsh tone warned both men who lost their grins.

"Okay. Just for the record," Blake asked, "how were you able to get close enough to watch the murder take place and fortunate enough to get away without being another victim? That's what dazzles me."

"Pure bloody luck and a little planning. I figured I'd watch and make sure it was Charli in the house, so I snuck up from the beach and approached from the front. There were bushes around the house to take shelter from being seen."

"You must have arrived after the killer had disengaged the security system by hacking into it or the alarms would have sounded."

John shrugged. "I guess so. Nothing happened, no lights or alarms, not like this place. Maybe I wasn't close enough to set them off. Though it's fortunate I had binoculars. Don't see so good with this eye anymore." He pointed at the sightless blue one on the left. "I'd thought to bring them so I could identify Charli before blundering up to some stranger and scaring the pants off her."

Blake laughed. "So now we have you at the right house. And you've explained what happened. There's just one more thing, John. Why were you so long coming forward? The murder occurred hours ago."

"I know. It's been eating away at me. There's no doubt in my mind that the lady died after she took a bullet in the forehead, but I really wanted to get the police there in case of a miracle, you know? Except, after I ran away, I tried to get help from the neighbors, and they weren't home. They had a pergola in their yard where I decided to catch my breath. Problem is, I kinda dropped to the floor after my marathon across the beach."

Charli spoke up. "Grandpa..."

"I know, kiddo. I wasn't thinking. I was too busy recuperating. Of course, I fell asleep."

Charli added, her glance at Blake a warning not to pursue this line of questioning, "Just like any ninety-year-old would have after what you'd been through. What I want to know is... how did you get back up to your feet?"

"Very slowly and painfully. That took me the longest. But once I came to, I knew I needed to get to the police station. After what I'd seen, I had to make a report."

"Okay. So, can you tell us exactly what it was you saw?"

"I saw this white guy, scary-looking creep, beat a woman nearly to death before he shot her. That's what I saw."

Chapter
Thirty-three

While the shock of John Madison's words wore off, Blake fell in love. That old man moved him so much, he felt affection for him flow throughout his whole body and nestle inside his chest.

He welcomed it. To meet a man like John Madison, whether he belonged to Charli or not, had to be one of his greatest privileges.

He never knew either of his grandfathers and his own father had been unapproachable on his best days and a patsy on his worst, always giving over to Blake's witchy, red-headed mother. He'd had some good times with him, but none that were unforgettable. Blake knew he'd never forget this day.

Meeting this guy, seeing how he interacted with his granddaughter, how much he adored her, well it broke down some barriers inside him, ones he'd formed over the belief that, in general, most people only cared about number one. And in his profession, other than a few worthy partners on the force, the general public he mostly dealt with didn't dissuade him of that concept either.

Watching Charli crouched next to John while he enjoyed Blake's own chair and petted the head of the woman Blake loved like he'd never loved another soul, John Madison made his mark. And Blake Sebastian now had two people he needed to protect.

Hold it... make that four.

Chapter Thirty-four

Angie pulled Kayla away from the doorway they'd been lurking behind. Using hand signals, she pointed to their bedroom and headed in that direction, knowing Kayla would follow.

Once they'd entered the beautiful, soft pearl-gray room with lime accessories where moonlight flowed in from the bay window overlooking the garden, Angie closed the door.

She dragged Kayla over to the bed where they both sat cross-legged on the quilted white cover. Grabbing a brush left on the nightstand, Angie crawled behind Kayla and began pulling the bristles through her long hair, something she knew Kayla loved.

"Tell me." After hearing what Charli and Blake had been talking about, Angie wanted answers.

"Tell you what?"

"Everything."

"I can't. You heard the same as I did. Charli and I are in witness protection. It's a secret."

"Kayla. I'm here with you now, and I'm not going away. Don't you figure I have a right to know who is stalking you guys? Like, I'm in danger too, right? So, spill."

"It doesn't work that way, Angie. The less you know, the better. Charli will send you away. I know she will. There're no good choices here. Back in Seattle, they made it very clear that I couldn't tell anyone about this. No one. That means you. Not if I want to keep you safe."

"Shit, Kayla." Angie cussed under her breath. "Hold on. That's not even your real name."

"It's going to be after this is all over. I want to make it legal. I like it, don't you? It has a nice sound... Kay-la."

Gently, Angie smacked her with the brush. "Quit changing the subject." Then she continued to stroke Kayla's hair rhythmically. "You saw some guy killing someone, you and Charli, and now the murderer is coming after you. Is that about right?"

"No. Charli didn't see it, just me. And quit probing."

"Right. I remember now. Charli's a Fed. She's your protector, your handler, babysitter, or whatever they call people who take care of the underage kids in these kinds of situations."

"Charli's my sister."

"No, Kayla, she's not." Angie threw down the

brush and yanked Kayla around to look her in the face. "She's just a cop doing her job."

"No. You don't understand."

"Yeah. I fucking do. I thought she cared about me when she beat up the sick slimy bastard. Crazy me, I thought I mattered to her."

"It did. You do. How can you question that?"

"Because now I know she's a cop. She was just doing what she gets paid for."

Anger exploded over Kayla's face, and her eyes stared daggers. She pushed Angie, almost off the bed. If the other girl hadn't grabbed onto the headboard, she'd have tumbled over.

"You listen to me, Ang. Charli broke protocol to help you. She left me alone in the car, knowing it was against all the rules, just so she could deal with your stinking life. She didn't have to. She chose to."

A small chunk of the iceberg lodged in Angie's gut diminished, but only a little. "Fuck!" She hit out at the bed, her fist punching once and then again. "I'm all fucked up."

"Yeah, well you're not the only one who's fucked up, Angie. Things are not always about you." Kayla slid her fingers through her hair in the front and tossed it back over her shoulders, a habit she had whenever she felt under pressure. "It's not Charli's fault that I ran to her place the night I saw the murder. *I* involved her in this mess. Then I insisted if they wanted my testimony in court, only Charli could take me into custody. It was all me, not her. Everyone's in danger because of me. I should just go out there, let that son of a bitch shoot me and save someone else from getting killed." Crying harder, unable to stop, Kayla hid her face, the tears drenching her hands and running over, dripping onto her legs.

Scared shitless now, seeing the avalanche she'd begun with her demands, Angie scrambled up next to Kayla and wrapped her arm around her shoulder. She started crying too. Something she hadn't done for many, many years.

Once she'd given up hope of ever escaping her miserable existence, the tears had stopped, replaced by so much anger that she'd often wondered how her body still performed when everything inside felt blocked, rock-hard... completely and utterly frozen.

"I'm sorry, Kayla. I'm a shit. Just ignore me."

"You don't understand. I met Melissa, the agent who died. She looked after me when Charli had some business, and she was really nice... and now she's dead."

"God, I'm sorry, Kayla. Come on, stop crying, okay? If you get me started, I'll never be able to stop." Angie swiped her eyes with her arm and patted Kayla, unsure of how to hold her or comfort her. That behavior wasn't precisely in her bag of tricks. "You're special. Of course, Charli wants to protect you. And Blake. Even me. That badass bag of shit has to come through me to get near you, you know what I mean? And that ain't never gonna happen."

Kayla sniffed and let her head drop onto Angie's chest. "You know what's so funny? I saw him kill that poor woman with a gun. After I saw the damage it did, I thought I hated them. But, when Charli left me in the car, I took her weapon out of the glove compartment, and I felt safe. I had no freakin' idea what to do with it, other than to point and shoot, but I finally felt in control."

"So, we get us one. I know a kid in school."

"Really?"

"Yeah, sure. You know the gang I hang with. They aren't exactly on the principal's honor list."

"You can say that again."

"Most of them scare me silly, too. And they were my only friends. Sick, ain't it?"

Then Kayla asked, "Why do you hang with those losers?"

"Hey, those *losers* don't hassle me. They just accept who I am. If I went up to Jorge and asked him to get me a gun, all he'd care about is the money. There'd be no questions, no judgment. Lately, I've been thinking of buying one and shooting Hank, the sick, slimy bastard. Just didn't have the cash."

Kayla's face dropped. "Right, I bet their expensive."

"Oh, yeah. You want one the cops don't know

about. They cost a shitload."

"Where would we ever be able to find enough money?"

"I don't know. But we'll work on it. With the two of us, we should be able to come up with something, right. Even if we have to steal it."

"I've never stolen anything in my life, too afraid of the consequences."

"I have. It's easy. I'll teach you."

Just then they heard voices in the hallway, and they snuck to open the door just enough to hear what Charli was saying.

"It's okay, Gramps. Blake sleeps on the sofa in the living room, not in his office. You heard him."

"I heard him say he'd ended up sleeping on it many times. I took it to mean he'd passed out on it. Which leads me to believe this is his house. Which bodes the question – What the hell are you doing living here, in *his* house? And... I might add, why are the girls—"

"Gramps! Enough. All your questions will be answered after we get some sleep. Right now, it's almost morning and you need to rest. Come on, now. Be good and—"

"Hey, kiddo, don't treat me like an old invalid. I can still throw you over my knee... Well, maybe not throw, but I can urge you in that position and paddle your behind good."

Charli laughed and both the eavesdropping girls had to cover their mouths to stop the giggles. They closed the door so as not to get caught.

Angie asked, "Did you see his wink?"

"No, when."

"Just now. The old guy knew we were there. I saw him wink at me... us. He's sure different than most old people I ever knew."

"Do you know a lot, because other than strangers, I sure don't."

"You're right. I never actually knew anyone that old."

"Me either, but I kinda like him."

"Funny thing, I do too. Maybe he can help us."

"You think he'd loan us the money?"

"Not if we told him what we wanted it for."

"So we lie. I'm really good at it. Leave it to me."

Angie saw Kayla's questioning look and smiled with as much innocence as she could muster. Kayla's response wiped the smile off.

"Don't try it on Charli. Trust me, she'll know."

Chapter
Thirty-five

Charli knew Blake would be waiting to discuss Poppa John's testimony with her. And as long as he stayed focused to that topic, she'd go along. But first, she needed to take a moment to think, rebuild her defenses – calm down.

With everything she'd gone through over the last twenty-four hours, her resistance was weak. No way did she have the strength to handle any pressure to carry on where they'd left off earlier in the evening.

She still hadn't gotten over the shock of how she'd ignited in his arms. God knows, it had been a long time for her since she'd allowed any man to get that close. And even then, it had been under her rules, her choice of when and where and with whom.

And never, not once, had she allowed any guy to get past her barriers. After the nightmare she'd suffered as a child, the only man who rated on her I-give-a-shit monitor was her Popsicle. And she was fine with that, always had been.

Now, at a time when she was so messed up, and her life was in shambles, her stupid heart had to decide to crush out on a womanizing asshole who thought females were put on earth for his pleasure. He didn't give them a chance to matter. He dumped them first, according to Candy and her warning.

Shit! Why can't I catch a break? Protecting Kayla was one thing. She'd accepted that responsibility. Taking on Angie, well... she had no idea why that kid had gotten to her, but she had. So much so that she hadn't been able to ignore her heartbreaking story, couldn't shrug it off with the old adage – not my problem. Hell, she could have gone to Blake and gotten him to handle it through the proper channels.

But that would have only made things worse for Angie. She needed to see the sick, slimy bastard getting some of his own shit back, needed to know she'd been vindicated, had gotten revenge. Once she saw the bottom-feeder, who'd made her feel lower than scum, forced to his lowest common denominator, maybe she'd be able to move on. Swallow the hate – drop the guilt every victim in her position suffers – and learn to finally love and respect herself for the first time in her life.

The one aspect Charli hadn't taken into

consideration, and should have known better, was that Angie's dependence would now be on her. Hadn't she ordered it so? *–The kid's coming home with me, moving in.*

Involvement in the Silverado case provided enough excitement; why in the hell would she take on more, and in her condition? Where had those words come from? Why hadn't she thought it out before going all rogue... Superwoman?

She'd broken Angie loose, sure. But now she owed her.

Dummy!

A quick scan and she knew she'd do the same thing again.

Quit procrastinating and get to the point of why you're hiding in this bathroom.

Because, she didn't want a replay of the hot mess she'd gotten into with Blake earlier. The time had come to shut down that freakin' gap and crawl back behind the wall to safety.

She stared in the mirror and saw her wild curls tumbling all over her head. The blonde color threw her. Like her gramps, she missed the red, and wished she hadn't felt the need to disguise herself before leaving Seattle. Too late... she grabbed the small combs she used to keep control and swept the sides up, not caring that small swirls escaped and clung to her cheeks.

Next, she added more makeup, eyeshadow that gave her brown eyes, still filled with a soft, gentle light only her grandfather merited, a hardening effect. Supposedly the windows to her heart, she needed them to appear professional, uncaring... unavailable.

Adding a thick coat of red lipstick, that she hoped implied a barrier, she sauntered out to the kitchen and found him missing. Her glance took in the sofa and saw that he'd left the coverings for a bed, but he was nowhere to be found.

Then she looked toward the patio and saw the figures of two men conversing. She recognized his Lieutenant, Bill Norton, with Blake in deep discussion.

Her heart sunk. What in God's name has happened now?

Chapter Thirty-six

Blake came into the house in time to see Charli brewing coffee in his fancy machine, and he nodded when she pointed at the cup. "Yeah, thanks." He rubbed his face and ended up threading his hands through his hair to link behind his neck. Then he twisted from one shoulder to the other, exercising his muscles. Finally, he moved toward her, full of intentions.

Charli retreated and her withdrawal left him under no illusions. Any personal headway they'd made earlier was completely gone. Her unmistakable warning threatened. Plus, the intimidating glare she'd thrown his way spoke volumes.

Back off and don't touch!

For now, he'd respect her boundaries, but sooner or later, they needed to talk. His patience had limits. He wanted her – something fierce.

"Is your Grandpa settled?"

"I think so. I gave him the pajama bottoms you lent him. He held them up to see their length and muttered, "He's a big boy, ain't he?""

Blake laughed and brought his coffee to the island where she now perched on a stool. Aware of her fragility, not wanting to push her buttons anymore tonight, he took a stool across the counter so he could see her eyes. Sitting there, he wasn't crowding her.

"Thanks for letting Gramps stay in that room. I respected that you'd left it locked. Kayla and I hadn't bothered with it because we had no need for the extra space."

"Yeah, well, the only reason I'd locked it was because with it being my office, and the cleaning lady not allowed in there, it became pretty messy – as you no doubt noticed. Once we'd decided this house would be the perfect safe-place for you and Kayla, I didn't have the time to tidy it, or remove my target gun cabinet, and so I thought it best to just lock the door. Now that I'm here, and your gramps needs a place to sleep, I have no problem opening it up."

"Are there a lot of guns?" A worried look had appeared as she zeroed in on the question of safety.

"Not now. I took most of them out to put in my trunk. I left two smaller handguns in the bottom drawer. The safety code is 1147 in case you need to get in there. While I was storing them, I got the latest report from Bill Newton, my lieutenant."

"I'll remember that because we used to have a post office box numbered 1147. By the way, Newton knows about our witness protection, doesn't he?"

"Yes. Besides me, he's the only one. But how did you figure that out?"

"He knew enough to bring Gramps here. A man off the street saying he witnessed a murder would get their attention, but no way would they have brought just anyone here to you. I figured his surname might have rung a bell."

"You're right. Good thing Bill was the first person our sergeant called in the department to approach John, and not Dudley."

"Dudley, the cop Gramps was so disparaging about. I'm sorry about him being so frank. He can be brutally honest in his opinions sometimes, and he took a disliking to your detective."

"Hell, he's not the only one. But, the man stays just inside the boundaries of my patience, and as long as I don't back up too often and bump into his lips, I'll leave things as they were before I took on the role of Major."

Laughing, Charli finally decided she couldn't stall any longer. "What else did he say?"

"We finally got the report that they found Mark Crawly. It took them a while. I guess the girls who usually check on your grandfather at bedtime saw the lights were out and a man sitting in his chair, covered and sleeping. It wasn't until later the next morning that they came to offer him a breakfast tray because he'd missed the meal when they realized what had happened."

"That it was Mark, not Gramps."

"Yeah. John must have covered him with a blanket and everything looked fine until they shook the body to wake him up. That's when they called the police."

"Poor old folks must have been shocked when they saw officers streaming into the place."

"I have no doubt." He thought about the uproar a murder would have caused at a senior's home like the lodge... their worst nightmare. "The authorities assumed he'd been assassinated by Silverado even before the crime scene investigation. Same silver bullet, same forehead shot."

"Was this before or after he'd ransacked my place?"

"What makes you think he was at your place?"

"Stands to reason... he found out about the lodge, didn't he?"

Blake didn't want to answer her. He knew what would happen. If he tried protecting her, she'd be pissed, the same as any other law professional. He had no choice. "It was after."

"Shit!" Suddenly pale, she bit her lip. "I thought I'd cleaned out everything at home that could possibly lead him to the lodge. I'd passed on my boxes to Mark, who'd promised to get me a storage unit until this nightmare ended." Charli turned away but not before he saw her eyes fill with self-loathing.

He couldn't stand her beating up on herself. "Honey, they had guards posted to make sure he didn't get inside your apartment, but they screwed up. Supposedly, they were called away on a bogus break-in complaint, someone with a broken window mysteriously having been opened. That's when they missed him. Otherwise, they'd have stopped him from getting anywhere near your stuff." First, he hesitated and then decided to get it over with so they could move on.

"According to Deputy Chief Prowler, you had a photograph on the wall in the entrance hallway where the frame had been smashed and the picture stolen."

Charli's hands fisted, and she shook her head. "Dammit, dammit... *Goddammit!* How could I have been so sloppy – so stupid? Of course, he'd see that. It was last year's Christmas masquerade party. Gramps went as Santa Claus."

When his eyebrow lifted, she added, "I went as an FBI agent. They had the lodge's banner above where we'd posed. And... they had our names listed."

"That explains why he didn't realize he had the wrong man when he saw Mark."

Her head dropped to the table. He couldn't help himself. Seeing her suffering, her pain, and sensing she'd hate his arms or lips; he just let his hand gently ruffle the curls on top of her head. "Please, Charli. Don't be sad. Mark Crawly was a good cop. He would have protected your grandfather in any situation, you know that."

"I do. That's what makes it so bad. Don't you see that?" Her eyes were teary and pools of sadness lurked under the anger. "I screwed up."

"Hold it. You'd just come off a brutal assignment, stressed out to the max and got thrown into a murder case. No time to even breathe. You're not a super hero, just a woman doing the best you can. And in my opinion, and that's a professional one if it matters, you've done an amazing job. So, quit disparaging the woman I happen to ad... mire." He stopped the word adore from breaking loose, but just. That term was on the tip of his tongue because it boomeranged in his head, flooded his heart and wouldn't be shut off. *He absolutely, forever and ever, adored her.*

"All I know is this. Crawly wouldn't have talked. So, Dylan Ross, the murdering bastard, had to have found out about my trip to Fort Lauderdale from seeing the material Gramps had scattered all over the living room. The old dear had been so excited about our vacation, that he'd gotten all kinds of printouts of the rental house and Fort Lauderdale tourist photos for bragging material to show off to his friends."

Charli lay with her head sideways on her arms, her voice rough as if she had trouble breathing.

"There's one thing I don't get."

"What's that?"

"How did he know for sure that Alicia Shoal, the witness, would be with me? How did he know that she'd been taken into witness protection?"

"See, I knew you'd eventually get to this question. And that was the other piece of news Bill shared. Seems like your supervisor, Deputy Assistant Jake Crompton, was found tortured and killed in his home also – before the break-in to your place. And this time, we believe the murdering bastard threatened Crompton's family."

"Oh, sweet Jesus. Jake's little girl, is she okay?"

"Yes. Her nanny had taken her to a friend's birthday party but they were due home about the time he took the bullet. Jake must have been frantic that she'd be Dylan's next victim. He put up a fight, but in the end, he talked. Thank goodness he didn't know where you were going."

"He knew we were together."

Blake nodded; glad she didn't insist he share everything. The horrific details, he kept to himself. "Right. He did."

"And he told Dylan."

"That's what they've determined."

Charli's direct stare gave him no leeway for making up a story. "So far, the lunatic's killed three people to find us. He's coming for me and Kayla."

"Oh, yeah. But he only knows you're in the city. He has no idea where."

Charli's stare caught him and drilled through the bullshit. "He's a genius for finding these things out though, isn't he, Major Sebastian? It didn't take him long to find Agent Dale, did it?"

Blake's nerves tightened from the sarcastic conviction in her voice. How could he argue the truth? He finally reached across and slid his hand over hers. "We're making arrangements to move you all as soon as possible. But in the meantime, if that prick finds this place, we'll be waiting for him."

***

Blake hadn't taken it personally when Charli flicked his hand off hers and left him at the island. She'd said goodnight first, checked each of the four security monitors on the one big screen, and disappeared down the hall.

Seeing the early beginnings of the sunrise through the patio window, he kicked off his shoes and laid down on the sofa, his pillow bunched up under his head.

Life had become insane ever since he met Charli. At first, she'd intrigued him, which seemed like such a watered-down, completely frivolous version of his attraction to her at the moment.

He remembered how it had been between them earlier, the explosive combustion as soon as their lips had touched... Good God! His true feelings now were like a pure gold bar compared to a tiny speck of sand.

He flipped over and put the pillow over his head,

foolishly trying to block out images that were floating around inside and couldn't be extinguished.

Rankled, disturbed, he swore he heard a noise and yet no one could have entered the house. Rising to his feet, he took the flashlight he kept in the coffee table drawer in case of a blackout and slowly tiptoed up the hallway.

He glanced in the girls' bedroom and saw them tangled in their individual blankets, together on the same bed with only their hands touching, linked.

Then he went to his office, intending to check on John Madison, a man who he needed to talk with, to pry secrets from... to understand why Charli behaved like a man-hater.

The door slid soundlessly and the sight he saw broke that last piece of resistance he had to loving a woman more than himself.

Charli was huddled in the uncomfortable office chair, slumped over, asleep beside the sofa bed where her grandpa lay snoring. He had no doubt she guarded the one precious person who she loved more than *herself*.

Chapter Thirty-seven

Blake started breakfast for everyone the next morning, showing off his cooking skills. Pleased but not surprised, his helper, Charli's grandpa, knew more about cooking than he'd ever learned from the culinary shows on TV he sometimes watched.

The two worked together, he cooked the bacon and eggs, while John whipped up some of the best blueberry waffles he'd ever tasted.

The five of them sat around the breakfast table, pretending a nonchalance that soon became real. Poppa John, as Charli called him, told stories about the old folks at the lodge that had them all laughing, and the relaxing atmosphere did more for their morale than anything else could have.

Soon, after tidying their places, the girls decided they needed to catch up on some homework since Charli refused to let them go to school. And Charli retreated to the gym off the master bedroom, declaring she needed to work off the two waffles she'd devoured.

Left alone with the person he most wanted to question, Blake opened the conversation. "John, I hope you're willing to help me understand Charli better. She's beautiful, great with the girls, and a cop I'd be proud to have on my team, but there's a definite hand's off signal that blares whenever I try to get close to her."

John chuckled. His good brown eye held a conviction that threw Blake for a loop. "Hell, son, she can recognize a hound dog when she sees one."

Taken aback, not sure if he should be offended, Blake questioned, "What do you mean, hound dog?"

"You know blasted well what I mean. A playboy, woman's man, operator, call it what you will. You're a high flyer, boy; you've got your ATP pilot's license, no doubt about it."

If John didn't have a big grin on his face, Blake would have been insulted. He sensed the man teased, but with a serious streak of intention, letting him know he was no man's fool.

"Charli's got baggage like most women today. But her baggage is hers, not mine to share. I sense it matters a great deal to you so I'll not tease anymore. Just know this; my girl can smell a fake from a mile away. The fact that she's let you get close goes in your favor." John narrowed his eyes and his tone hardened. "If you're her match, then you better treat her right. Man to man, you mess with her and I'll shoot you where you dangle, see if I don't. Now tell me how you're going to keep those girls safe from that scumbag who wants them dead."

Before Blake formed a comeback, his cell rang, and it was the ring tone for a call he had to take. "Thanks, John, for being honest. I'm not playing around with Charli, so you can put your gun away. I'm in so deep; no other woman will ever satisfy me now."

"I know. That's why I never punched you in the nose when I first entered the house. I may be blind in one eye, son, but I see real good out the other."

Chapter
Thirty-eight

Kayla waited until John was alone to approach. "Mr. Madison, can we speak with you for a few minutes?" She gestured to the bedroom where Angie waited at the door, grinning a welcome.

"Not if you call me Mister again. You girls either call me Poppa John or Gramps, like Charli, that's if you want me to be your pal." He put out his hand for Kayla to take, waited until she slipped hers into his and walked her to the room.

Angie closed them inside, and then pulled the lime green chair over to the bed for him while the two girls sat cross-legged on top of the white cover.

"Charli told me a little more about your predicament last night. How she's looking after you both. She takes her responsibilities seriously so you can rest easy. Now, what can I help you ladies with?" Kayla watched John's arms rest on the chair, and his hands grip each other loosely.

The man's face had more natural color than most of the elderly she'd seen, which gave him an appearance of a healthy person. His white hair shaved close to his head and his bushy eyebrows, tamed by a barber's trimming, made him kinda adorably cute.

His confidential demeanor and his cheeky grin, as if they were sharing secrets, delighted her. She couldn't stop the swell of affection that consumed her, and looking at Angie, she saw the other girl's eyes shine with liking, something that didn't happen often. Normally, they were freaky empty.

"You know why Charli and I are together, don't you?" Before he could argue, Kayla admitted, "We listened at the door last night."

"Oh, I know you did."

Kayla, stunned at first, had to laugh. "You're scary for being a blind man."

"There's an old saying – *there's none so blind as those who won't open their eyes and pay attention.* I might be blind in my pretty blue eye but that old brown one sees a lot more than most people are comfortable with." He turned to Angie and spoke very gently, "For instance, I know you've survived hell and are terrified to go back there."

Tears appeared before Angie could recover from his words. "I ahh, I... ahh, yeah. It fu... freakin' sucked."

"I bet. But from this day on, kiddo, everything will be okay. Know that inside your heart, in your belly and everywhere else you need it to lodge. You belong to me and Charli now. And you, Kayla – you too. From this point on, we're family. So, I'm your grandpa, and I'll do whatever I can to help you. As long as we stay..." He held up both hands and wiggled them... "as close inside the law as possible."

Kayla hugged him, she couldn't help herself. Charli had shown her just how sweet that kind of connection could be, and she needed to pass on that sweetness to the old guy.

Angie sniffed, and her words came out loud, cruder than intended. "We need money to buy a gun."

Chapter Thirty-nine

The day passed slowly for Charli, catching up on her paperwork and exercising, running away from her demons and finding them beside her on the treadmill.

She had to stay away from Blake. Her defenses were screwed; he'd gotten through once. And after her earlier discussion with Poppa John, she feared he'd break through again.

***

That morning, when Gramps woke to see her in the chair next to his bed, he'd sat up and made room for her to snuggle against the wall next to him.

"You shouldn't have stayed with me, kiddo. I'm fine. You must have been uncomfortable, sleeping in that dumb ol' chair."

"I wanted to be close by. You had some pretty nerve-wracking experiences. I was scared you might react."

"Or maybe you were hiding from Blake."

"Excuse me?" Stunned, she glared at him.

"Sweetheart, don't give me the evil-eye, and stop fighting it. Blake's a good man. He can make you happy. Give him a chance."

"You don't know that, Popsicle. You only met him yesterday."

"In person, yes. But, that's the first time I've ever seen you look like a woman who'd just felt joy in a man's arms. Don't give me that glare. I can tell when two people have just been together."

"We weren't."

"Tell that to someone without a brain and one good eye. Besides, I listened to his partner brag about the guy all the way over here. And, I saw the infatuation plastered all over his face the minute I stepped through the door. He's smitten."

"What you didn't pick up on was that he's a love 'em and leave 'em kind of guy. I've already been warned by one of the women he's left."

"At least he's honest and doesn't purposely break their hearts." When she gave him the how-the-hell-do-you-know kind of look, he admitted, "His partner might have also mentioned that the women in town flock to him like bees to a honeypot. Besides, isn't that kind of your scenario? How many men have you dated over the years with no intentions of letting them get close?"

"That's different. I needed to focus on my

career."

"Bulltoodie."

"Grandpa!"

"Then quit lying, kiddo. You've been terrified all your life to let any man get close." He held up his hand. "Anyone but me. And I don't count because I'm family. Besides, I was in your life before the accident."

"Don't talk about it." She stiffened. The desperation in the suddenly hard tone she used normally kept him off the subject.

"Why not? Because it makes you cry? Because it scares you?"

"Because it fills me with so much sadness that it takes me days to crawl out again."

"Look, Charli. You've played that angle with me for the last time. I'm not gonna let you get away with it anymore. I never should have from the beginning. You have to face the fact that the accident wasn't your fault. So, you called for your dad to look at the pretty tree, and he hit the deer and went off the road. It was an accident."

"But I caused it. And they both died. Only I survived."

"Sweetheart, you're no longer a child. Look at it from the angle of your dad or your mom. Would they have wanted you to live in purgatory because of that moment? You suffered enough, spent all night alone down in that gully with a broken leg, crying and scared, not knowing where you were or what had happened. Isn't that punishment sufficient for even a harsh judge like you? A ten-year-old little girl, Charli. Think of it. Enough! Give yourself a break. Quit being such a coward and open the door to your heart."

"Oh, Gramps, do you really believe I've never fallen in love because of that day?"

"Yes, to put it bluntly. Yes. I believe you've refused to feel alive, to love and be happy. How could you, when you thought they'd lost their lives because of what you did?"

"Poppa John!" He'd never been so brutally blunt before.

"Face facts, Charli. Most of your life, you've lived with that hideous belief. And it's torturing you, keeping you in a prison of your own making. You need to open the cell, kiddo. You're the only one with the keys."

Charli's eyes filled; tears on the brink of overflowing. "You sound like the department shrink. She accused me of something similar, hiding myself in my job and not living life fully, blah, blah..."

"Well, her blah, blah was dead on, my girl. Do me a favor and think about this. I don't want you to let a good man get away when he's so ripe for the picking."

Charli wiped her eyes and giggled, glad for the comic relief. "Oh, he's been picked over a number of times, Gramps."

"Maybe, but has his seed ever been planted?" He chuckled mischievously.

Totally giggling now, Charli punched his arm gently, swung herself off the bed and winked. "I should have known you'd get to the essence of what this is really about, your ultimate desire for a great-grandchild."

**

With her head still full of the advice her gramps had shared, feeling punch drunk, she needed some space. Why hadn't she admitted her fatal secret, given her gramps all the truth? Shying away from that question, she wondered if she had purposely kept people from getting too close because of a fear she'd lose them. Is that why she's kept that emotional wall up between her and anyone of the opposite sex?

Her hands gripped the bars of the tread mill. She'd run for miles with those words haunting every step. No matter how fast she went, she couldn't outrun the message. Was it time to open her jail cell and step out into the world of love and families, marriage and babies?

Could she?

With Blake?

So far, he'd been the only man who'd ever made her want to.

Chapter
Forty

Kayla was scared. It was almost suppertime, and she knew Charli wouldn't accept her lies for much longer. Poppa John and Angie had left the house over two hours ago to buy Jorge's gun, and they still hadn't returned.

When the girls had brought up their idea to the old man, he hadn't scoffed. He'd taken them seriously. "How much?"

Angie spoke, "I know a guy, Jorge, who can get us an unmarked one but it's over five hundred."

"Bucks?"

"Ahh... yeah. Like, I know it's a lot of money, but me and Kayla, we want to be able to protect Charli if that asshole comes looking for us here. He's done a lot of shit to get this close, who says he won't keep killing people until he finds out about this place?"

"You want to protect Charli? Why not yourselves?"

Kayla answered without hesitation. "Because, when he gets here, she'll be out in front of us, you know that."

Pops had nodded. "You figure the killer's that smart?"

Kayla spoke up. "Pops, the police in Seattle gave me a kind of report on him, and he's one bad dude."

"Okay then. Can you get a hold of this Jorge guy?" He turned to Angie.

"Yeah. I have his number. Look, I've thought this out carefully, and you both need to know that I'm the one who has to go and make the deal."

"No. Not alone." Kayla's automatic response had Angie in her face.

"Yes, alone! You can't leave the house, not with that rotten prick after you. At least while you're inside, he'd have to come through Blake and Charli to get to you."

"Blake left, he got called out for a while." Poppa John's deep voice cut through the squabbling.

"I'm going alone. Just give me the money and cover for me. I'll be there and back in an hour."

"Oh no you don't, little girl. Either I go with you, or the deal is off."

Angie's shocked surprise didn't quite cover the glimmer of relief hidden deep in her eyes. "You're too old."

"Screw that. I'm not too old to call an Uber. Nor am I too old to make sure the gun's in working condition and not a piece of crap. And I'm definitely not too old to blab if you don't take me with you." His smirk enforced his comments. He meant business.

Kayla now regretted giving in. How in the world had she ever let herself be talked into this stunt? It seemed like such a brilliant idea at the start.

Having Charli's gun, holding it for that little while, she'd chilled out, had control. It felt like no one could mess with her because she had protection... power. That ultimate high was the reason she'd started this disaster.

She checked her phone again and saw no new messages. The last text she'd received said they were approaching the house where they'd planned to meet Jorge to exchange the money for the gun. Angie had even sent a snapshot of the dump with the street sign showing in the background.

But that was more than an hour ago, and though she'd texted Angie at least a dozen times since, she'd gotten no answer.

She left the room and found Charli frantically swimming laps in the pool, as if driven by forces too hidden to understand.

Chapter
Forty-one

"Gramps, he'll be back." Angie paced the small, dirty room from one end to the other. The overwhelming smells from dirty paper plates full of leftover pizza and dried-up sushi, plus the empty beer cans scattered high and low might not have been so bad if the two standing fans gave off cold air and didn't just swish around the dead, hot stink surrounding them.

"How do you know he'll return? We trusted him with half the money, but the original deal had been for him to have the gun waiting."

"He needed the cash so he could buy it. It makes sense."

"So, he lied on the phone. The gun only costs two hundred and fifty. The rest is for his – what did he call it – his time and trouble." John spoke with a Spanish accent that sounded surprisingly like how Jorge had spoken. "What says, he didn't lie when he said he'd be back. The kid's got my two hundred and fifty bucks, and he's disappeared, left us in this pigsty. We've waited almost two hours. I say we cut loose and call it a bad plan."

Before Angie could answer, they heard the door open and slam closed. Jorge and a friend had arrived, both swaggering and both either drunk or high.

Angie felt the revulsion instantly with fear crowding right behind. Now what? Scared, but playing the game, she stepped forward. *Don't show any fear or they'll love this even more.*

"Where's our gun?"

"She-et! I told you they'd want the gun, didn't I, Ramon?" He shoved his friend's shoulder in a playful, drunken way. "And, we'll get it, woman, but the price is a bit higher than we discussed. I need another four hundred."

John stood and pulled Angie close. "Then the deal's off. How about you just keep the two hundred and fifty I already gave you, and we'll just leave."

Jorge rushed at John but Angie got in-between. Lifting his arm in John's direction as if to slap, he snapped, "Hey, old man, how about you shut the fuck up?"

Angie kept him from connecting and got a backhand for her tenacity.

Just then, Charli, a cold mask of fury emblazoned on her face, stepped into the room from the back of the house. "And how about *you* back off, asshole, and give the money that you took from my girl and my grandpa back to them? That sounds like a helluva lot better idea to me."

Jorge's jaw dropped. He swung to face his friend who also wore a stunned look. He turned back to her, furious indignation engulfing his face.

"How'd you get into my place, bitch? The back door was locked."

Ramon's instant agreement followed. "Yeah, cop. You broke in."

"So, sue me. Now, give back the money." Charli stood; legs wide and her hands on her hips, pure defiance plastered over her uncaring expression. "You don't wanna play nice? We can do this a different way – it's all the same to me."

Without another word, Jorge dove at her, his fist up and ready. Perfect for her to grab and use to swing him around, head first into the wooden frame of the doorway. The crack of his skull sounded like he'd be suffering from a blistering headache after he came to.

Charli turned to the other dude who'd stood dumbfounded. Amazement and disbelief flashed across his face. Not willing to play nice, he reached for a gun stuck in his belt.

Like she was going to give him time to get it loose? No way.

Her fist drove into his face so hard that he went ass-over-teakettle across the room. She followed, watching him try to get to his feet. Before he came to a full stand, she kicked his legs out from under him and planted her heel in his forehead. Out cold, he didn't move when she reached down and took the gun dangling halfway out of his belt.

Charli turned to Angie who'd stood in front of John, holding him back from getting involved.

Angie had seen Charli's cold, single-mindedness when she'd taken on Hank. That had impressed her. But now she saw the rage of a person who'd been pushed too far. Now she wasn't just afraid for herself, but for the man who'd suddenly decided he wanted her as a shield.

Tense moments passed as she waited for Charli to let loose. But the only words she spit toward them as she shoved the gun in front of her were, "Is this what you paid for?"

Chapter Forty-two

Dinner was tense that night. Blake didn't understand why everyone tiptoed around Charli, but he found himself doing the same and not knowing why.

Once it got to the point where she'd grunted a negative response to Kayla, who'd held out one of the take-out Chinese containers, he'd had enough. He'd seen the girl's worried face fill with sorrow, tears being blinked away.

Glancing over at John, who'd been mostly silent, acting like a puppy with his tail stuck up his ass, he lifted an eyebrow, silently questioning.

John just shook his head and looked down at his plate where he'd pushed the food from one side to the other without much of it getting to his mouth.

Blake checked out Angie and saw that the same girl he'd met days ago had returned, the one who'd lived in misery, and it came off in waves from her sour attitude. She'd disappeared for a little while and her replacement had been a sweet kid.

What the hell happened while he'd taken time for the job?

After the disturbing news he'd gotten earlier, he couldn't stand the friction here, too. They needed to clear the air.

"Okay, gang, what's up? You're all acting like the world's on the brink of war, and Charli's the one with the red button."

The three doghouse culprits looked at each other and then peeked at Charli who didn't lift her head, just kept shoveling food into her mouth and chewing. Silence cut through the tense atmosphere until all you could hear were the stupid annoying wind chimes by the pool next door.

Blake felt his annoyance turn to anger. He banged his hand on the table, and just as he'd intended, everyone jumped. "Listen, we're all under a lot of stress, so I'm not gonna get too annoyed. But we need to stick together, talk about our worries. Not turn all quiet and moody." Staring directly at Charli, he waited for her to break.

No one moved. The smells of the sweet and sour pork balls hung in the air, interacting with the strain oozing from the girls and the old man. Finally, Charli lifted her head and pointed first at her grandfather, her finger shaking with suppressed emotion.

"You're an idiot."

"Dammit, I said I was sorry, Charli. For the tenth time, I'm sorry already. It seemed like a good idea at the time."

"A good idea?" Her voice sat one octave higher than a man with his pecker in the grip of a maniac. "To go along with Angie and buy a fu – a bloody piece of shit gun from scumbags like those two? You're kidding, right?"

"Look, sweetheart—"

"Oh, don't you sweetheart me." This time Charli's tone sunk, a snake slithering on the ground kind of low. She shoved her chair from the table and went to stand next to the cowering old man. Blake watched him shrink from her fury, and not knowing what the hell they talked about, he nonetheless had to stop her from carrying on.

"Charli! Enough. I said we should talk over the situation not intimidate and yell."

Suddenly, as if his words had broken through her passion, Charli's face cleared and her expression changed from anger to fear. Her voice shook with so much pain that they all sat frozen.

"Don't you understand, Popsicle? If anything had happened to you, because of me, I'd never be able to live with that. You've got to know. And you two," she pointed at Kayla who was openly crying now and then to Angie who'd somehow moved to stand protectively beside her friend, "How could you have put yourselves in so much danger?"

"I wouldn't have let anything happen to Poppa John, Charli. I swear." Angie's white face and wobbling lips told their own story.

"So you'd have let them beat on you, is that what you're saying? It was close, Angie, so close. I've never been so terrified in all my life." Her voice finally gave over to the tears she'd been forcing behind her fortified wall, but once it crumbled, nothing could stop the flow.

She doubled over, holding her stomach. Her moans scared Blake as much as they seemed to terrify the rest. God, if the woman broke, if her PTSD finally forced a breakdown, they'd be sunk.

He knew what none of the others did. The killer had found out which school Kayla attended. It was just a matter of time before he came for them here.

Though Prowler and the Seattle team had finally sent instructions for the next safe house, he feared it might be too late.

Stepping close, Blake picked Charli up in his arms and thanked God when her arms tightened around him, and she hid her face in his neck.

John rushed to caress her shoulder but stopped, sensing he needed to let Blake take care of the situation. He embraced the other two instead.

Blake nodded his reassurance to the small huddle, and then he carried her to the master bedroom for privacy and peace. They needed her to be strong again. She was their pivotal force, their mainstay... the person they all loved.

Chapter
Forty-three

Dylan Ross only concerned himself with one thing. He didn't give a rat's ass about people or justice or love. He cared about his reputation. It's what he sold to the bigshots who hired him. What earned him the millions he'd come to expect.

All his life, a bi-racial male who'd been insulted and condemned for his color from both sides, he'd vowed to be rich, in control and respected. In the beginning, he'd tried doing things according to the rules, the way society says it must be done.

He'd gone to school, followed the rules, had even worked like a dog to go to college and get his law degree. There, he found he had more brains, more intelligence and a hell of a lot more balls than most of the white dudes in his class.

Those superior assholes who'd always condemned him for being poor orphan trash were lazier and dumber. Here, in the place of higher learning, they taught him his biggest lesson. His race didn't matter near as much as his class, or lack of it. Power earned respect, and money gave one power. Life lessons 101... he passed with honors.

Once he had his license, he proudly went from door to door, applying for work, thinking he'd be a bonus for any law firm. What he found out was that they'd take him for low-paying, low-level positions. Swallowing his pride, he settled for one, gotten on the ladder, and would have begun his climb – except for one pivotal incident.

He'd been celebrating his first position with the most prestigious establishment in Chicago, and he'd been pulled over by cops who neither listened nor gave a shit that their rotten attitude and vicious abuse violated his rights.

The more he tried to quote the law and stick up for himself, the more they beat him and tased him. By the time they'd hauled his ass to jail, he'd suffered massive bruises, a broken ankle and fourteen stitches to his head where one of their boots had left an imprint.

Of course, after they charged him with a DUI, which registered one point over the legal limit, and assaulting a police officer, which he never did unless arguing was now a form of assault, he ended up for the first time in his careful life, busted.

With no money, no friends and a crooked system that only saw his blackness, he had eleven months to decide how he would overcome and carry on.

In the can, he'd met up with knowledgeable gangsters, one of whom knew of a guy, a cold-hearted killer who everyone feared and many had hired. He told stories about this dude, tales that resonated with Dylan, whose real name was Diggs.

He'd never known his last name, and so they'd made a joke at the orphanage and called him White – Diggs White. In college he'd changed his name to Dylan and after they released him from prison, because his hair had turned silver before he'd taken to dying it, they'd nicknamed him Silverado.

In prison, he'd pulled off his first kill, hired by a skinny gay man as his protector, and he never looked back. For years he'd performed only those hits he needed to keep him in the money he'd become accustomed to. His meticulous planning and numerous skills with technology had worked in his favor.

He'd never been caught because he made sure he was never seen, like a black shadow, in and out, job done.

Until Seattle. He'd been in a hurry that night, sloppy, not thinking about open windows. The light had been off when he'd first broken into the apartment, he'd been hidden. The bitch had turned it on just seconds before she'd stepped around the wall. He'd been there in full sight and had no option but to take the shot rather than to let her react, scream, warn the neighbors.

And look where that got him – up Shit Creek without a fucking canoe, a paddle or an excuse for his stupidity.

Because of one moment's improbable odds, he now had a witness on the run. And since he hadn't taken the time to disguise himself in any way, the bitch could ID him. Fuck, one stupid decision to just get it done, and look at the fucking mess.

He knew how to add makeup, change his hair coloring, choose accessories – hell, he'd used every variable when it came to camouflage. Look at him now, wearing a police uniform he'd stolen from the dead cop he'd left lying on the floor of his apartment after he'd followed him home.

When a person was willing to kill at random, nine out of ten times, he'd get away with it. So far, he'd been lucky. He'd killed the FBI bigshot; the old man he'd thought was Carolina's grandfather and had turned out to be Crawly from the SPD, and the lady agent whose bad luck was to be in the house that Carolina Madison, Special Agent for the FBI, had rented. And now, this rookie schmuck, who just happened to be his size, had paid for that crime.

The uniform had gotten him into the high schools and allowed him to bullshit the information out of the Vice Principal about the list of new students. His phony story about a woman kidnapping her stepdaughter from the girl's father had worked like a charm – that and his badge. He'd gotten the list of new female students from each of the schools he visited. Lucking out on his second try, he knew instantly which girl fit his Asian-American profile and the new name she had chosen, Kayla Steele.

Then he'd spent a few minutes hacking into that school's database and he now possessed the street and house address where they were holed up.

He holstered the cop's Glock 22 and made sure he also had the silver .45 Automatic tucked into his boot. His moto of being prepared had worked well in the past.

Now it was time to get this bit of foolishness over with and return to his regular routine. Next on his list – Kayla and her bodyguard, and that job would be a pleasure.

He'd shop the next morning and head back to his Air B&B with a new costume and make-up. He was thinking a nice old white dude out for a stroll while scoping out the joint wouldn't draw any attention. All he needed to do now was get a dog, buy a cane, and gather info about the layout of the house.

Chapter
Forty-four

Charli suffered massive shame over her complete breakdown. Embarrassed, horrified at how many tears she'd shed before Blake managed to soothe her, the only noises now were the occasional hiccups, sniffs and sighs.

Inwardly writhing in mortification, she questioned her sanity. How could she have given such a display? Never in her life had she lost it so completely.

Sure, she'd had moments in the dark when she'd soaked her pillow or sat under the shower crying until the water turned cold. Who in this profession hadn't experienced such lows? Especially if they performed in the types of cases they assigned to her – the undercover gang infiltrations – both dangerous and necessary.

Thing was, she'd never had an audience... never. Controlled, hard-assed to the point where some even condemned her as being heartless, she kept it together, kept the shitty stuff to herself.

The only soft moments, when she loved life, were those shared with her gramps.

The rest of her days, she lived like a regular person, had drinks with casual friends from the office, dated when she had the urge for sex, and excelled in the job she loved.

And now, entwined in the king-size bed with Blake, the shirt on his chest soaked, his hand playing with her hair, life had changed... because she had surrendered.

Not understanding just how much she'd shored up until the wall crumbled, allowing the pain freedom, she shivered. How had she ever managed her day-to-day life carrying such a heavy burden? Suddenly, words broke loose, words she'd never intended to share with another living soul.

"I killed my parents." She said it out loud for the first time and held her breath. The words hung in the air, stark and horrible. She girded herself for his condemnation and disgust.

Blake's sigh filled the darkening room. He shook his head, his reply spoken low and soft, "You didn't, Charli. Circumstances created the accident that killed them, not you."

She stiffened, pulled her head back to look into his face. She saw the gentle light in his eyes and fought to get away. She couldn't handle his pity when she expected censure... or in the very least, to be taken seriously.

Overcoming her resistance and gathering her in a tight hug, he wouldn't let her go. "Hold it, I know what you're thinking, and you're wrong. I don't pity you, a grown woman who should know better than to think like a dumbass. Who I feel sorry for is the little girl who spent the night alone in the ravine where she'd been thrown, a broken leg, and no one finding her until morning – only to admit that her parents had died. And... no one working the crash had even known she'd been in the car until they'd managed to contact her grandfather. That's who I feel sorry for. And, no matter how angry you get, Charli, I'm only human. I'll never be able to wipe away those sentiments. My heart is never going to accept that I can't feel what every living person with any compassion would feel – sympathy for that poor child."

"You read the accident report." She hid her face again.

"Fucking right I did." He tightened his hug, arms gently putting pressure to cuddle her closer. "Baby, I needed to know everything about the agent who was involved in a case in my city, especially after Prowler warned me you might need support. He's a good cop, thorough and with sound judgement. After he'd hinted at a background I might want to check into, baggage you'd carried for years, I'll admit to doing the research."

"My memories are cloudy. It's like my shame

refuses to let me see what happened. I've always believed it's my punishment for saying what I did."

"You pointed out the beautiful trees."

"No, that's what everyone believes. The truth is that I undid my seat belt because I was reaching for my mom's camera. That's the reason they didn't see the deer. They were helping me find the *fuck-ing cam-er-a*. I wanted to take pictures of those... those beautiful, godforsaken, son of a bitchin' trees." Her voice broke. Overcome with shame, she hid her face again.

Blake shook her gently. "Oh baby, would you condemn any other ten-year-old for doing the same? Like when our children do silly *kid* things, will you be heartless and turn your back, sentence them to a life of unforgiveness?"

Charli heard his words. She'd listened with her heart in her throat, praying he could give her the magic she needed to get past the horror, the confession of her real crime.

As his words filtered through her brain, a wall crumbled and she began to see herself again as that little girl in the woods. *Once she'd come to, the descending darkness had terrified her. Foreign noises filled her imagination with images of cougars and bears, all hungry for the 'meal of the day', little Carolina Madison.*

Horrific pain had kept her immobile. Crying heart-rending tears, calling for her parents' help, unable to scream because of shock, unable to help herself or them, she was engulfed in pure unadulterated misery. When she finally did hear the sirens and faraway voices filtering through the darkness, all she'd heard was – "it's too late." That's when she'd prayed for death and mercifully passed out.

"Charli? What are you remembering? You've gone very pale and you're shaking. Baby?"

His edginess penetrated and shocked her into replying to what he'd said earlier. "I'd never treat anyone like that. I couldn't."

"But you are, Charli. Tell me why you feel it's okay to treat little Carolina Madison that way."

"I don't... I wouldn't. Oh my God, but I do."

"Yes. You do. You've closed your heart to the small girl who begs to be forgiven."

This time the tears were healing. She cried for the years she'd betrayed the defenseless child in the woods, refusing to see her cruelty or the true reality rather than the obscene one she'd clung to.

Blake lay beside her the whole time, his arms a haven of shelter and protection. He hadn't condemned her. Instead, he'd listened and defended her.

She lifted to a sitting position and found tissues waiting in his hands. Thankful for his consideration, she mopped up her face and lay over on her back, empty and lighter than she'd felt in years.

Full darkness had descended with only the shining moon to give them enough light to see one another, an indication of how long they'd been squirreled away in the bedroom.

She thought about the others and guilt began to manifest. "I need to apologize to Gramps and the girls."

"No, Charli, you don't. They love you and understand that you were frightened for them because you care so much. You can make amends in the morning, tonight is for us."

"What us?" She smiled as she taunted him. After sharing such heavy secrets, her heart had lightened. Now, she wanted to laugh, to dance... to make love.

Her mind remembered how tightly their bodies had meshed together earlier. How they'd fit so perfectly. She slid closer and began kissing his face. "Suddenly, I feel lighter and happier than I can ever remember. It's wonderful."

"I'm so glad, Charli." He smiled, looking relieved, his charming grin contagious.

She laughed. "I need to do something fun. Hey, I have an idea. Wanna screw?" The words were supposed to sound playful, a reflection of her sudden lightness of heart.

"Uh uh, Charli. No screwing between us." He yanked her back into his arms after her instant withdrawal. "Either we make love, or I leave right now."

Stiffening, she replayed his words... *make love.* Was he trying to tell her something? Her poor muddled head couldn't properly assimilate the hidden meaning; he needed to spell it out.

"You want to make love to me?"

"No, baby, I want to make love *with* you."

"Oh well, since you put it like that, then sure, we'll make love to each other."

"The thing is honey; you can't *make love* unless you actually love the other person. See, if you don't, that's when you have sex, kinda like what I've been having all my life. But with you, it's different, because you – I love."

Sensations she'd never experienced before exploded, starting in her brain, speeding into her heart and plummeting with the biggest explosions in her lower stomach. Aroused beyond anything she'd ever known, cascades of ecstasy unfurled.

He loves me. She had to tighten the muscles in her groin because the need there detonated. *He knows my secret and yet he really loves... me.* A feeling of utter warmth, such as she'd only experienced with her Poppa John, circulated from her head to her chest, slinking through the opening to her heart and blossoming... taking root. She'd never thought it could be so intensely beautiful, so utterly filling and so mind-blowingly blissful.

She took his face in her hands. "Then make love to me."

Almost rough, he pulled her closer. He stared into her eyes, his totally open and revealing. She returned his gaze, telling him without words that she needed him, wanted him and... completely and utterly adored him.

***

Blake had never known fear as he'd suffered while waiting for her reaction. Watching Charli assimilate his words, their meaning, he held his breath and didn't move a muscle. Putting everything on the line, knowing he'd walk away if she hadn't been able to give him the answer he needed had been the most terrifying thing he'd ever lived through.

But now, joy had overtaken those fears, and he scooped her close, kissing her with every ounce of love he'd saved all his life to give to the woman he'd choose to be his wife.

While his hands worked at her clothes, pulling and tugging at the material, needing her naked body next to his, his lips travelled over every inch as it came into view. He couldn't stop from idolizing her beauty or exclaiming over and over again how much he cared.

Starting at the point where he'd removed her shorts, he exclaimed, "Oh baby, am I ever going to love you here." He nuzzled her entry and heard her breathing quicken.

Not wanting anything to end too soon, he moved upward to where she'd already taken off her blouse. He gathered her breasts, kissing each nipple and caressing their fullness. Again, her gasps urged him to hurry. He reached for her lips where he made love until she arched upwards to accept his fullness, her signal that she wanted more.

Only, he wouldn't be hurried. He'd waited too long for this moment and he needed it to last. To be special.

"You're perfect, baby. Perfect. I love everything about you." He softly kissed her lips. "I especially love your mouth."

His hands gathered her hair on each side of her head to keep her where he wanted her. "And your hair drives me crazy, did you know that?" He leaned back so he could ruffle the softness. "I love blondes with curls and big brown eyes."

"It's not blonde."

"Excuse me?"

"My hair, it's not blonde."

"You know what, I don't care. I'd be crazy about you if you were bald."

This time, she grabbed his hair in both fists with serious intentions. "How about you love me with less words and more action?" Her eyes were alight with twinkling jest. "Then I'll take my turn to show you the parts of your body I most like."

"That does it! Hold on, baby. Hold on tight."

Chapter
Forty-five

Charli held on and had the most mind-blowing experience of her life. The man knew all the tricks of how to satisfy a woman. He'd lifted her arms up above her head, holding her hands, entangling their fingers and made free with every area he could reach. When he focused on her breasts, he not only laved them with his tongue and sucked on the nipples; at the same time, he plunged deep inside her.

His kisses and snuffled breaths on her neck and tiny bites at her ear made her squirm in delight. Taking the time to whisper his delight with her tight wetness, he swiveled his hips to get deeper. "You're so wet, baby. You can't know how good it feels, how hot you are."

His passionate thrusts while he kissed her lips, sucking the essence from within, drove her to the brink. The man had a body he'd worked hard to make strong and muscular. His thighs against hers were proof that he cared about health and strength. He made her feel feminine and delicious.

She allowed him free reign, and he'd taken over completely. In her normal relationships, she'd always been the rider, the in-charge person, but not with Blake.

He had full control and his way of performing left no doubt that was the position in which he excelled. When he lifted her legs higher to give him better access to her sweet spot, she lost it completely.

He rammed her with his body and at the same time with words of love that added the missing connection she'd never known.

Soaring to heaven, she experienced a climax that left her throbbing with joy. Hoarsely, a sob broke loose as he penetrated the slickness one last time, thrusting powerfully, his fullness pumping, pulsating... passionate.

Needing to give him as much pleasure as possible, she tightened her inner muscles and again rode the wave. Oh, God! It felt so good, so perfect.

Soon, floating back to earth, she totally and forever gifted him with everything she had to give.

Chapter Forty-six

Waking from a snooze, Charli found the bed empty. She laid there for a few moments, wondering where Blake had disappeared to. The coolness from the air conditioning blasted, driving her to search for her clothes. She found them piled on the floor by the bed.

Before she could dress, Blake appeared with a tray of heated Chinese food that smelled like ambrosia. "Oh no you don't. You're not leaving yet. We need to eat, talk and make love again. I haven't come anywhere near to getting enough of that delicious body you flaunt around here all the time."

Charli let go of her shorts, and instead, she reached for the shirt he'd flung on the floor. "Okay, I'll just borrow this. The air conditioning is making me cold."

He stared at her hard nipples poking against the

blue material and grinned. "I see that. And so you know, that's just become my favorite shirt."

"Down boy. And bring that food over here. I never ate much earlier."

"Are you kidding me? You were the only one shoveling food into your mouth while the rest of us sat in misery."

"I never tasted a morsel. Was I that scary?"

"Yep. Like a sixteen-hundred-pound ravenous gorilla in the middle of the room. One nobody wanted to mess with."

Charli giggled. "You're exaggerating, shame on you."

He put the tray on the bed, held his hand over his heart and posed. "On my honor."

Suddenly serious, she leaned forward, her worry apparent. "I know I was upset, but I never meant to make anyone afraid."

"Honey, you didn't just scare them, you... ahh, you terrified them. It was the huge sign written over your behavior that screamed a warning – I'M ON THE EDGE! The others realized they might have been the obstacle that pushed you over. It's a dreadful scene watching the person you love fighting so hard to keep it together."

She thought about his words and went to stand. "I need to apologize right now."

Stopping her, he said, "Don't. I just checked on everyone and they're all out for the count. It's been a crazy day for them too. They need to recuperate.

It'll wait until morning."

She watched his expression and knew instantly. "Something's wrong." She put down the chicken wing she'd snagged and wiped her hands on the napkin he'd thoughtfully added.

"No. Yes. Well—"

"Blake Sebastian, I'm still the agent in charge here. Spill it."

He handed her the two filled wine glasses before they spilled and snuggled onto the bed beside her, moving the tray between them. Then he chose the fattest chicken wing and held it without taking a bite.

"Can't we wait until tomorrow before we let reality back in? Trust me, it's not the end of the world, but the news isn't good. I promise I'll explain in the morning. For now, we're all safe. I have an army of officers positioned around this joint. No one can get past them."

She stared into his beseeching face and asked, "You promise there's no immediate danger?"

"None. Tomorrow is soon enough to make some changes. Please, Charli."

Charli had already heard about the new plans and felt confident that things would work out just fine. "Okay. Tomorrow we'll move to another state's safe house, which will make the data he collected null and void."

Blake turned to the dresser by the bed and reached for his wine, nodding and at the same time speaking words that sounded as if he'd said, "That's right."

Charli didn't like him dodging her gaze while mumbling a nonsensical reply, but she let him get away with it because she'd never enjoyed such a wonderful encounter and she wanted it to last.

Still, her mind did warn... *Something's up.*

Chapter
Forty-seven

Waking to a man in need, tucked in front of him, cuddled close and totally engaged in delightful morning sex, Charli contributed fully. Warm skin nestled behind, arms strong and persuasive, whispered words urged her on. She allowed him passage and reveled in their combined mounting passion.

When he whispered his thank you in her ear after their mutually enjoyable finish, she'd smiled and thought no one else would ever be so thoughtful. Drifting off again, still feeling heavy after her sharing from the night before, she snoozed and didn't wake until she felt him leave her side.

"Blake, come back here. We need to talk." She tackled him before he could disappear. Wanting to hold him to his promise of giving her the complete lowdown of what happened yesterday, why he'd been absent a lot of the time, she stopped his escape to the shower by following him there and joining him.

His engaging grin and soft kisses weakened her enough that she went along with soaping his back and letting him soap hers, but only after he promised to come clean... a pun he thought hilarious... when they were finished.

As they dressed, he explained about his absence the afternoon before. Only the murder of one of his own cops would have tempted him to leave the house.

"I didn't know where you'd disappeared to, one minute you were there and the next, Gramps said you'd been called away."

"Detective Newton figured I'd want to be involved, and he was right." Further explanation of what he'd witnessed shook her foundations.

"Dispatch took a call from the rookie's girlfriend who'd stopped by his place and found him. The officer, Tom Sheldon, had worked the night shift, and he'd promised to take her out to eat, go shopping, and then he would catch up on his sleep afterward. Except, he hadn't shown up, nor did he answer his phone."

Charli listened to every word, but his expression warned there was a shock coming.

"The girlfriend, angry that he'd broken his word and fallen asleep, went over there and let herself in, only to find him shot, lying on the floor in his underwear."

Charli listened closely. "Where was he hit?"

"Forehead, dead center."

"Aww... shit!" Her angry reaction reignited the worry she'd put aside for the last few wonderful hours. "It still could have been a coincidence. He might have disturbed a burglar. Was anything missing?"

"Just his uniform."

"What?" Charli felt the fear building, the instinct that this wasn't an ordinary act of violence. "So, you don't believe it to be a typical break-in gone wrong. Was he shot with his own gun?"

"No, with the same gun that killed the bartender and his two customers at Freddie's."

"Jesus. It's him."

"We believe so."

"He wanted the uniform so he could get close to this house."

"We thought of that so we made sure our guys all wore their civilian clothes last night and hung back. We wanted him to stand out. But, since then, we've changed our minds as to why he needed the uniform."

"Why?"

"Bill Newton's daughter goes to the same school that Kayla goes to, and when he picked his girl up after the final class yesterday, the Vice Principal visited with him, congratulating the police department for hiring such gracious and polite officers like the one who'd been there earlier asking questions about a missing girl. We had no one assigned to any such task."

"You're kidding me? So now that bastard knows we're here for sure and where Kayla was going to school. Thank goodness we kept her home yesterday."

"Remember, he's also skilled with computers; enough to use his own to shut down the security system at the house where he shot Agent Dale."

Charli's mind raced through the points and arrived at the same conclusion Blake obviously had too. "He hacked into the school's computer system and accessed their student database."

"We checked the log files and someone had infiltrated their data. We followed the trail and found out that he'd used a computer at the library. He'd cleared the browsing history but our guys were able to track his path. When we asked for the video surveillance, we were told their camera had been fiddled with yesterday. The one taping that area had only covered the far wall rather than the day's traffic or individuals who'd been using the equipment close by."

"He's too smart to show up on a camera. If he hacked into the school's files, it was for one thing only."

"Yes. He now knows this address." As he buttoned his shirt, Blake started to turn away. "She's not going back to that school."

"You're bloody right. She's not going there or anywhere else in this city. We need to get her away from here."

"Yes, but…"

Chapter
Forty-eight

"What do you mean, but? We have no choice. I won't put her in danger. Jesus, Blake, she's just a kid."

"Don't you think I know that? I love her too, Charli. She's a sweetheart and nothing is going to happen to her, I swear. We've made plans."

"Plans? I'm not sure I'm going to like this."

"Prowler has talked to my superiors, and they've agreed that we need to stop that maniac here and now. As you've been told, no one has ever been able to get close to him. Christ, they've never had any real leads... until this situation."

"They want to use her as bait? Is that what you're telling me? I won't be a part of that, Blake. Not for her. Besides, that would bring danger to everyone in this house. The man is resourceful, committed and kills indiscriminately. We not only have Kayla to protect, but Angie and my grandfather."

"That's why we've come up with a plan to secret you all away from the house without anyone knowing."

"I'm not leaving you."

"We have jobs to do, Charli. Those kids, and John, need you. They trust you. I'll have my men, and we'll stage a set-up to lure him inside, and then we'll nab the son of a bitch."

"Is that before or after he puts a slug dead-center in your forehead too?" She stomped out of the room in search of her girls and her gramps, fury riding her hard. Before she stepped into the group around the kitchen island, she took a deep breath, relaxed her shoulders, and drew her curly hair up higher on her head, digging the combs into her scalp on purpose.

As soon as she showed herself, the laughter stopped, the girls circled the old man and the three stood as if awaiting their sentence.

"Really? It's you three against the big bad ogre now? So, I'm sorry already. I acted like an ass yesterday. My excuse could be massive PMS, except it isn't."

Her grin accompanying the comment made all three relax and smile.

"You," she pointed at Angie, "you scared the crap out of me, little girl, taking such dangerous chances with your safety." She held up her hand to stop Angie's retort. "Don't. I know what you're going to say, and you're wrong. Even if my goofy gramps hadn't been with you, I'd have still felt like my world was ending when I saw you put yourself in front of that maniac. Hell, kiddo, I don't know how it happened, but the truth is this. You matter to me. Bigtime matter! I meant it when I said we'd be together from now on, so get used to it."

Charli watched the metamorphosis taking place, hardness dissolving into hope. The girl believed her. Then Charli saw her grandfather slip his hand into Angie's and squeeze.

Good.

Next, she swung to Kayla and spoke with conviction. "You've gone way past being my job. You're mine now too. You have to know that. Right?" She waited for Kayla's smiling nod, and she smiled in return, their eyes holding long enough for the message to be sent and received.

Then she attacked the old man wearing the goofy grin. "And you, Popsicle, you will be doing penance for a long time until I forgive you for taking chances with my precious grandfather."

John moved closer, chuckling and playing along. Since she'd just used his own words back on him, he knew what to expect. "So, kiddo, what's my punishment?"

"A big hug, and if you throw in a kiss, it'll be a start."

***

Blake arrived just as she had called out Angie, and standing in the background, he waited before interrupting the family scene. It struck him forcibly between the eyes. If he wanted Charli, she wouldn't come to him unencumbered. He'd be taking on a rather large family.

After she had her say and was enclosed by all three in a laughing group hug, he waited to step forward for his share.

Searching his conscience, he looked hard at just how these latest circumstances made him feel. Other than he couldn't wipe the dumb grin off his mug, or block the glow in his heart; for the first time in his life, he sensed he belonged to a loving family. He swallowed the sob, blinked rapidly and joined in.

Chapter
Forty-nine

"Okay everyone. You're all on board, right?"

Blake had just sat the group down and given them their instructions about escaping from the house without anyone being aware they'd left. "Let's go over the plan one more time."

"The pool cleaner's van will be pulling into the driveway as close to the fence as possible. He'll be opening one of his back doors. Just in case our perp has eyes on the house, we'll be sneaking you all out wearing the same cleaning uniforms."

Kayla spoke up. "What uniforms? They wear shorts, muscle shirts and a cap."

"Exactly. You'll be wearing their clothes, so when you go to the van, you'll be identical. There'll be three pool guys waiting in the vehicle in the same outfits – our men of course."

He looked around the room and saw the confusion. "Follow me now. When the first pool guy comes out to work on the pool, he'll go around to the side of the house to fiddle with the system; he'll slip into the house and pass on his clothes to Charli. Dressed like him, she'll take his place. She'll head for the van, get inside and the second fellow will be waiting to go back out to the pool and start cleaning, dragging the net and so on. After a little while, he'll need to go to the shed and Kayla will be waiting to take his place. She'll head out to the van for a bag of supplies, and the next cop will be waiting. Then we'll do the same with Angie. Once you've been replaced, you ladies will hit the road. Charli knows where the safe house is, and my men and I will wait here for our man to show."

"Hold it. What about Poppa John?" Charli's eyebrows lifted and a stubborn glare appeared. "You're not expecting him to stay here for the fireworks, are you?"

John reached over to rub Charli's arm soothingly. "Charli, I've been taking walks every day since I got here. No reason I can't take my walk and not return, is there? I could meet up with you in the van after you girls are free."

Charli didn't hesitate to argue. "You've only been here a couple of days, Gramps. It's not like you've been walking for weeks. And, we didn't know then what we know now. Dylan's closing in, probably watching the house as we speak. We can't take any chances."

"Oh, pooh! What's he want with an old man. Why I was just out earlier this morning before the rest of you even stirred, and I met this nice old guy walking his dog. I told him I'd meet him after lunch while he took his dog for his afternoon stroll. Couldn't I tag along with him for a distance and then just stop at the marina coffee shop at the end of the street? You could pick me up there, right?"

Blake looked at Charli to see if this worked for her. He saw her indecision and decided to push it. "Sure you can, John. That'll get you to safety. If Dylan's watching, it'll look like we're going about our business as usual. We can have someone tagging you if it'll make Charli more comfortable."

Charli still appeared indecisive until John nodded and winked. "See, little girl, easy-peasy!"

"Look, gang. All we need is for our perp to believe Kayla and Charli are still holed up here, thinking they're safe. That's why I've had all my men back off. They're around but not visible anymore. What time did this old guy say he'd be around, John?"

"He mentioned he takes a nap after lunch, so he said around two. I told him I'd watch for him then."

"Okay, I'll have our guys set up the switch at that same time, and we'll clear you all out before tonight. If he makes a move, I'm betting it'll be after dark when he thinks the girls are alone and sleeping."

Chapter
Fifty

Precisely at two, the pool cleaner's van arrived at the back fence and Charli and the girls were waiting to make the costume change with each of the undercover police women that were assigned to the case. Dressed as the normal pool cleaners would, in shorts and t-shirts, caps securely on their heads, they followed the plan.

John stood watch at the front door. As soon as he saw his new friend and his pooch arrive, he strolled out to meet them, and they ambled off together.

First, Charli did the quick change, pulled the cap well down over her hair and strutted out to the waiting van, followed by the other two teens. In no time, they'd made the exchange and were headed to the coffee shop to pick up John.

Kayla spotted him just as they were arriving, and Charli decided to hold back until the other old fellow left before making a move.

"Let's just wait until he's alone. I don't want to call any attention to us in any way." She pulled over to a parking spot on the side of the road and turned off the motor.

No one thought anything when John began walking their way, his friend at his side. Charli knew when her gramps made friends he could go overboard in his welcome.

Her old Poppa John liked everyone he met until they proved to be unlikable. Only then, did he drop them. When she questioned him about his faith in people, he gave her his this-is-a-lesson look and said, "When I meet a person, it's with the expectation that they're good people. When they prove me wrong, my trust disintegrates and I back away. But sometimes, you know, you have to give folks more than one chance to prove their mettle."

His philosophy in life had always been – nobody's perfect. If you have low expectations from someone else, that's what you'll always receive from them in return.

Only this time, they needed him to lose his new friend and just get into the van. Charli watched as he did just that. He'd turned to the white-haired, white-bearded fellow walker, shook his hand, patted the small dog standing between them and started to walk away.

Except, that's when his new friend dropped the leash, turned on him, held a gun to his side and roughly frog-marched him the last few feet to the van. The dog began barking, sensing a problem, and got kicked out of the way for his trouble.

John, realizing the crisis, screamed a warning, "Go, Charli, go." When he began to yell, the dog barked more and only John's struggling stopped the maniac from taking a shot to stop the yapping.

Charli grabbed her gun from under the seat where she'd stashed it and took aim; only there was no shot without endangering her grandfather, something she had no intention of doing. Once the men had gone past the side of the van where the walls were without windows, she had no chance.

Both the girls were screaming for the monster to let John go and Angie had opened her door, on her way to his rescue. Charli had to haul her back by the hair. "Stop it. Stay in the van." She didn't step on the gas, she couldn't, though everything about duty screamed inside her – you have Kayla... get away.

Kayla yelled, "No, Charli. We have to save Poppa John."

By then, the decision had been made. Both the men had climbed in the back of the van, Dylan shoving John to get him in, and even the dog had somehow sidled in next to John, huddling close to his side.

The lighter-skinned black man holding the gun pulled off his full beard and his old man's cap. He ran his hand through his tight white curls and wiped the sweat away. "Fucking costume's so hot, I could've stroked out. Let's go Agent Madison. I want us out of here or first, the dog gets it and then, the old man."

Charli stepped on the gas and headed back the way she'd come.

"Where do you think you're going?"

"You told me to drive, you never said where." Her voice could have solidified rain.

The two girls, seated in the front of the old van with her were crying, huddled together, Kayla secretly typing on her phone.

"If I see anyone messing around, I swear, it's game over. I'm sick and tired of dealing with this shit. Alicia, you should have minded your own business that night. Look what you've done now; everyone has to die because you're a nosy bitch." The resentment in his voice came through loud and clear. The man was not happy.

Within a short time, Charli watched in the rearview mirror and saw Blake's fancy Jeep pull out from behind a car and sneak into the lane next to hers. She felt slightly better, knowing she wasn't alone. But no telling what the maniac would do before he made them stop.

"I'm driving in circles here. Where do you want me to go?" She kept her voice level, hiding her relief.

"There're warehouses out by the airport. Head in that direction and while we're on the way, maybe say your prayers. You know what's in store for the lot of you. Truth is, I can't wait to get this over with and get back to the real world. You ladies have led me on one hell of a chase, so don't expect any sympathy from me."

Charli heard the thud as he kicked the dog, who had begun to whine. The poor animal screamed in pain, and John snatched him up in his arms.

"Shut up, you stupid mutt. Don't know why I picked you from all the others. You've been nothing but a fucking headache ever since I broke you loose from the pound."

Charli checked the rearview mirror and saw John cuddle the poor animal onto his lap, while the golden dog, who looked like a mix of terrier and poodle, shivered, eyes enlarged and looking as if they were full of tears.

"Right, you freak. Go to John. Think he'll save you? It ain't gonna happen."

John began to speak, rage apparent, but Charli cut him off. "Do as he says, Gramps. Just do as he says."

"Listen to your granddaughter, John. Oh, and Charli, if you want the old man to live one more second, you'll pass over your weapon. No way would any cop worth their wages be out here without a gun. And from what I've read, you're one of Seattle's finest." The sneer was unmistakable.

Charli reached under the seat, pulled out the

Glock and handed it over her shoulder. She saw Angie holding Kayla close. Tears dripped down Kayla's face, her behavior screaming – it's all my fault. I'm to blame.

Angie didn't cry. Instead, she secretly lifted her shirt and leaned forward enough for Charli to see the gun she'd hidden in her belt. One of the guns from Blake's cabinet.

Charli's stomach dropped.

Now the prayers began in earnest.

Chapter
Fifty-one

Blake couldn't believe Kayla's message that was staring him in the face. The old man with the dog had been their perp, and he'd been close to the house – right under their noses all this time.

He'd created a costume, gotten a dog and made friends with John, and he now held them captive in the pool boy's van. Jesus! How could he have let them leave? Turns out, they would have been safer if they'd stayed home.

He grabbed his car keys and headed for the garage. Just then, he saw the van go past the intersection at the head of the street, and he rushed to catch up to them, giving orders to his crew the whole time.

"Newton, I'm following a 1990 blue Ford van, license number four, nine, six, XRR, heading south on Highway ninety-five. Do not intercept. Repeat, do not intercept. Follow at a distance. It's

Dylan Ross and he's got four hostages. Do not spook him."

"Got it, boss. I'm connected with your GPS. We're heading out now and will be nearby in five minutes."

Blake closed the phone and wiped his sweaty hands on his pants, one at a time. How could he have been so cocky, thinking he had it all figured out. Forgetting that the original plan of sneaking the girls from the house had been suggested by Prowler, he put the guilt on himself and it fit like a snug coat.

He saw Charli's face, felt her last kiss, her whispered words that she kinda guessed she loved him. Her teasing grin when he questioned her, "You *kinda* guess? Baby, you either know or I'm gonna have to work on you again."

"Then for sure, I'm still guessing. Maybe if you try a little ahh... harder next time." The giggle that followed had him pulling her close for one more kiss that left them both breathless and heated.

The van stayed within the speed limits, making it easy to keep them in his sights. He wouldn't crowd too close because the backdoor windows revealed the upcoming traffic. It was safer to ride alongside a lane or two over. He couldn't take any chances that he'd get made.

Time passed with visions crowding his head. The two sweet girls playing games with Charli; sticking up for John when they worried that Charli would attack. His favorite memory – the night before when he held the strongest, bravest, most beautiful woman in his arms and told her he loved her.

Suddenly, he saw the van pull off the highway to the right. He had no idea where they were heading. Son of a bitch, the animal was taking them on the Cypress Creek exit, and onto Dixie Highway to the industrial area where they had a lot of old warehouses and buildings. Seeing as today was Sunday, and most of the buildings would be closed, no one would likely pay any attention. The image of his girls alone with no one to care launched such a vicious pain in his gut, it almost doubled him over. *Not on my fucking watch.*

He pulled his wheel hard, cutting back through traffic, forcing cars to give way, creating a hazard anyone without authority would pay a hefty fine for. Too bad – he couldn't take any chances on losing them.

By the time he'd made it through the traffic, the van was out of sight. Not wanting to be spotted now wasn't an option. He needed to find them fast.

Blake called in his position and had one of his men at the station give him the reading from the map they'd picked up by satellite. Thank God for up-to-date technology.

"The van is arriving at a building called Hal's Custom Marine Sewing, Blake. They're pulling in right now. It's a smaller structure where there are trees around the parking lot in front of the building. He had to know the business would be closed seeing as how it's Sunday."

"Find out who owns it; question them if Dylan's been anywhere near there recently. The man is smart and creative. He plans for every development. What better place to kill his victims than a warehouse that's empty for the day, then head off to the airport only a few miles away."

"You're close, Blake. Go another mile on 17th Street and right on Route 1. Pull over in the Cold Storage building's parking lot and go on foot from there; otherwise you'll drive into a trap. Back-up is on the way."

"Affirmative. We can't let him know we're onto him. Keep a low profile until I say different, got it?"

"Yes, sir. Understood."

Chapter
Fifty-two

Charli sent a signal to Angie by waving her fingers as if to say pass it over. The slight nod led her to believe she'd listen, but Angie was all heart, and she'd gotten very attached to Poppa John.

What if she decided to take the shot herself and risk them both getting killed? Charli couldn't stand the thought, and the stress she'd shed began to reassert itself.

Her foot started shaking on the gas pedal, and her heart double-timed so that swallowing hurt.

God, no. Don't let me lose it now. God!

The atmosphere, sinister and heavy, added to her reaction. She needed to say something, lighten the tension.

"Where are you taking us?"

"Just keep driving. There's a nice quiet shop a few miles further down that's closed for business today, seems that they're all attending a wedding.

We won't be interrupted if we stop there. And don't try any funny business."

"You can bet on it when you have my grandfather beside you."

"Good, because I might just take pity on the old bastard, he's a smart man. I like smart people."

"Then you'll love him. They say he's a genius."

"Just shut up and drive."

Charli kept her eye on the road behind, praying that Blake saw them take the turn-off. She couldn't see him anymore, but then neither would Dylan, which was just as well. He didn't seem to recognize Blake's vehicle while they were on the busy highway, but on this out-of-the-way street, he'd spot it instantly.

After all, it had been the vehicle she'd used to chauffer Kayla around from the time they first arrived. She just prayed he hadn't seen them driving it. According to the itinerary they'd set up for him, he only just found the house, so the chances were excellent he wouldn't recognize it.

She finally saw the older building where, no doubt, he meant for them to stop. Intense panic built rapidly. Her saliva glands began working overtime. Forced to swallow repeatedly to stop from hurling, her mouth became dry, her throat parched. The muscles in her stomach clenched, the pain so intense she feared she'd double over.

Afraid that the pounding in her chest couldn't go on much longer without her heart bursting, she let out a small moan. Her foot lifted from the gas. Angie's hand grabbing hers gave her a lifeline. She grasped it tightly, using her awesome will power to force calm.

"Why are you slowing down here? Keep going until you're in front of the shop and then pull in behind the trees."

Angie swiveled, her tone hard. "She's not well. Give her a few seconds. You can hold off shooting us for that long, can't you?" Angie's bravery sharpened Charli's wits. With the extreme strength of necessity, she came out of her funk.

No doubt, the fact that Angie had passed over her gun had a lot to do with it too. Now she felt back in charge... somewhat. She had the means to protect. She just needed the chance.

While she leaned forward to check on Kayla, who'd sat in misery the whole time they'd driven, sniffing occasionally, she tucked the gun out of sight. "You okay?"

Kayla returned her gaze and nodded. "Whatever happens, I'm so sorry that I started this nightmare."

Fed up with her remorse, Dylan raged, "You should be fucking sorry, kid. You've given me nothing but grief. Now this is the way we're going to play it. I've got my gun aimed at John's heart. Right? So you will all get out of the vehicle and come to the back of the van. Then you will circle around us as we walk to the shop." He hit John on his shoulder when he tried to wrestle away. "And you, you old bastard. If you give me any grief, I'll shoot your precious Charli, don't think I won't. She's been another huge thorn in my side. Now it's payback time and trust me, this will be enjoyable."

Chapter
Fifty-three

Blake watched the circle of people shuffle toward the shop and wasn't surprised that the killer not only had the key, but must have disengaged the alarm system the IT department warned him about. The asshole had to have some freaking fine tech skills.

Not knowing exactly why Dylan had gone to so much trouble to set up this far away shop, he could only surmise he'd intended to take John hostage and have Charli bring Kayla to him at this address.

If he'd been watching the house, which they now assumed he had for at least twenty-four hours, then he knew how many police were around. And he for sure knew that Blake, a Major with the Fort Lauderdale police department, owned the house.

They'd underestimated the asshole – not something they'd do again. In his gut, he knew Dylan intended to shoot everyone and walk out like nothing happened. Capable of doing just that, would it be better for his SWAT team to storm the place and pray they get him before he shot anyone else? Maybe get a sniper set up and hope to get a clean shot? Or should he try and sneak in alone?

Knowing he couldn't take unnecessary chances with the lives of the people he loved, he opted to go in first. If he didn't stop the massacre then his men, now strategically placed around the building, would deal with the lowlife bastard.

Taking the vest and rifle that Bill Newton had thoughtfully offered, he gave his instructions and began scrambling past the trees, behind walls and keeping low, heading to the back door where he figured he could enter.

As quiet as possible, he broke the bolt that kept it locked and forced it open enough so that he could slip through. When he got inside, he headed for the main area that housed seating sections from customized boats, many only partly covered.

Sewing machines were set up, a few with pieces still attached. Rolls of fabrics were stacked in the corner, various colors and styles of vinyl and leather, the air permeated with their strong smells.

It gave him a place to hide as he snuck closer to where he heard voices. Hands sweating, he took a deep breath and inched forward. He saw a small boat mirror and picked it up, slowly lifting it between two piles of newly covered pillows so that he could get eyes on the situation.

He saw that Charli stood in front, with the girls behind her. John, glued to Dylan's gun, was being held as insurance that no one would be stupid.

"Charli, lift your pant legs, then take off your shirt and turn around."

What the fuck?

Charli's face dropped, and she argued, "Why the fuck should I take off my shirt, you pervert?

"Because, as soon as I take my gun from John, you're going to make a move with the gun you kept for backup. We can't have that now, can we?"

"I gave you my gun. Why would you think I have another?"

"Because, in your place, I'd have brought one. Now lose the shirt so I can make sure you're clean."

He dug his weapon harder into John, who tried not to wince but couldn't stop the pain from appearing in his expression.

Charli lifted the shirt off and dropped it beside her. Then she turned and the weapon he'd expected became visible.

"See, you didn't disappoint. I knew you'd be carrying. Take it out of your waistband slowly and throw it on that pile of stuffing over there."

Charli did as she was told but took her time.

Blake saw the despair on her face and knew she'd make a move soon. In her place, he'd rush Dylan hoping to at least save the girls.

Before she could make her play, Blake sent a bullet through the painted window, giving his men

eyes in the room and his sniper a shot at Dylan.
Then he stepped out for a showdown.

Chapter
Fifty-four

Charli had known Blake was close by, she'd sensed his energy as if they were wired on the same wavelength. It had given her the strength to drop her gun as ordered.

But once Blake showed himself, drawing fire his way to take the heat off her grandfather, she had no choice but to act.

His ruse worked. Dylan let John go so he could take a shot at the man with the gun. The bullet hit Blake in his shoulder which forced him against the wall.

While this happened, Charli dove for the old man and shoved him down and behind a table while the two girls also took that moment to sprint around a finished panel waiting for pickup.

Unfortunately, she wasn't able to escape with her gramps because Dylan's fingers had snatched her hair, dragging her back towards him, effectively stopping Blake from taking another shot.

Though he'd gone down, he hadn't lost his weapon or the ability to kill. But Dylan's gun pointed toward a wriggling Charli... that changed everything.

Blake began a conversation, hoping to lure Dylan from behind the post and give his men the chance they needed. "You might as well give up, Ross. We have the place surrounded. Even if you manage to kill us all, you won't get away."

Blake had hoped his words would rile the killer and draw him forward. But it didn't work. What did work was the pooch nobody had remembered saw a chance to get to his friend. When John fell, he came out of hiding, scooted across the space and rushed to the old man on the floor.

The tense atmosphere had worked her up enough so that rather than being timid, her fangs were showing and the growls she emitted were fierce. When Dylan roughly went for Charli, she became incensed. And when Dylan lifted his gun for another shot toward Blake, she flew through the air and attacked.

Not only did her teeth grip the man's wrist but she'd forced the arm with the gun back so its aim was now to the ceiling.

Suddenly, a shot rang out and everyone froze.

Dylan flew backwards and slid down the wall, blood oozing from the wound in his stomach.

Whimpering, the mutt let go and ran to John.

Charli twisted around and stopped her fist from connecting with its projected target and instead, cautiously grabbed the fallen jerk's firearm.

Blake swiveled to where the shot had come from.

And Kayla, hair in her face, looking like an avenging angel, let her hand fall; the gun now at her side. Shaking wildly, the weapon slipped from her fingers and dropped to the floor.

Angie rushed to her and gave words to what everyone else felt. "Serves you right, you slimy son of a bitch killing bastard. Good for you Kayla."

***

Charli was the first to examine if Dylan was dead or not. Though unconscious, the pulse in his throat gave proof he was still alive. She then ran to Blake, who was slowly lurching to his feet, then sliding back to a sitting position. Holding his shoulder with one hand, he waved her off toward Kayla. The poor girl looked spooky, as if in a trance.

Angie had closed in, but she'd stopped from touching Kayla when she saw the bizarre condition of her friend, the paralysis, the spooky appearance of someone in agony... the white-faced, bulging-eyed shock.

Like a statue, Kayla hadn't moved, hadn't spoken. It was as if she'd held her breath and hadn't let it out. Her gaze fixated on Dylan, who lay spread-eagle on the floor, his hand holding his stomach as if in disbelief.

Charli's arms gathered her close and were the catalyst to bring the girl back. Sobs broke out, and she wailed so loudly, bumps formed on Charli's body and her hair stood to attention. Her hold tightened.

Understanding the cry released a lot of the terror the poor girl had suppressed for the last few weeks, she rubbed Kayla's head, smoothing back her hair, and whispered, "Shush, baby, everything's going to be okay."

"C-Charli, is he dead?"

"No. He's alive. You only gut-shot him, no less than he deserves. He would have killed us all. You know that, right? You saved us by what you did."

"I thought I'd killed him."

"No. He'll live to spend the rest of his life in jail. And we'll all be witnesses at his trial and get the satisfaction of putting the low-life away."

Knowing that Charli was who Kayla needed, Angie ran to help the struggling old man get to his feet. "Take my hand, Poppa John."

"Kiddo, that's not gonna be enough to get this old body upright again. You're just a mite; a good puff of wind could blow you over."

Pretending to be insulted, Angie groused, "Yeah? But I'm a really strong mite. Come on, let me help you." She put her shoulder under his arm and between the table and her support, John succeeded. The dog watched them carefully, making sure that the girl didn't upset her idol.

And once John stood steady, she ran to lean against his knee, shivering, whimpering in her joy to see him upright. Slowly, he bent over to pet her, and said. "You're a good doggie, my girl. It's Milk Bones for you, as many as you can eat."

Angie also petted the happy animal and agreed, "First chance I get, I'm buying her a big fat chewie bone and a stuffed play toy. She's wonderful, Poppa John."

He hugged Angie to him and added, "No better than my other girls. You are all heroes, especially poor Kayla." The two joined arms and walked toward where Charli and Kayla were still entwined.

Angie stepped closer to add her support. "You did good, girlfriend." She tentatively touched Kayla's back and looked pleased when the girl reached for her hand. "But you said you weren't going to take one of the guns after you knew I'd snuck into Blake's stash."

Kayla's grin was sickly, but a good start. "See, I'm a liar." She flipped her hair back over her head in her Kayla way. Then she looked toward where the EMT's were rushing at Dylan. "But at least I'm not a killer."

Charli laughed and ruffled her hair before moving to where Bill Newton stood next to his boss. He helped Blake rise after getting the signal and led him to the stack of pillows to use as a leaning post. Bill gave Charli the eagle eye, and in a mock-mad tone, he said, "The boss waved off the paramedics, Agent Madison, he said it's only a scratch. But the stubborn man needs attention."

"I'll make sure he gets it, don't you worry, Lieutenant."

"It's Bill, ma'am. Bill Newton. I'm very pleased to meet you at last." He held out his hand, and they shook. "It's a good day when a killer is stopped and heading for prison. Thank you for what you and the girls did."

"Like they say in the movies, it was all ad lib. Nothing went as planned."

"You're right. I've never seen anything like what just happened – an academy performance."

Blake grinned, "Meet my new family."

Chapter
Fifty-five

Later that night, Charli's gaze passed over her new family gathered in the kitchen, sharing the steaks that John had grilled for them on the barbecue. There'd been a lot of laughter and high jinx, reaction to what they'd all undergone that day.

After they'd released Blake from the hospital due to his insistence, everyone had been taken to the police department where they'd been interrogated – answering pointed questions, each giving their own accounts of what happened.

Since they'd done nothing inappropriate while saving their own lives, their individual statements were taken, and they were all released. Even the dog had come home with them.

At the warehouse and then later at the police station, the canine had freaked when they'd tried to separate her from John's gentle touch. Because of his persuasion, promising the dog would behave, they'd looked to Blake for approval, and let John keep the animal with him the whole time.

Even at the house, the pooch hadn't left John's side. Charli heard her Poppa John's gentle voice talking to the pet, helping her to relax. The dog allowed the girls near her, but still had a problem with Blake.

Could be his voice had a deep tone like that of a previous owner. No one knew, but her nervous reactions included slinking behind John when Blake entered the room, growling when Blake touched one of the girls and outright snarls when he embraced Charli.

"Jesus, the mutt hates me." Blake grieved while the others laughed at his fake distress.

"She'll behave once she settles down. Now that I think of it, she didn't like Bob, I mean Dylan, or whatever his real name is, much either." John picked up the contrary animal, and had his face lovingly washed for his trouble. "She put up such a stink at the police station earlier, that twerp, Dudley, had to behave while he had me in that cubicle."

"Gramps!"

Not in the least sorry, Poppa John winked at the others, adopted a fake pathetic attitude and answered, "I apologize."

Charli just shook her head, trying to hide the grin.

"You still haven't told us the dog's name?" Blake

interrupted, saving John from further censure.

"I never heard her referred to with an actual name now that I think about it. Dylan told me the dog had been in the animal shelter when he found her. She's quite young, not a pup, but not fully grown either; I'd say maybe a year or two old. When we return her, they should be able to tell us."

Charli rushed to the chair where he sat with the shaking bag of bones on his lap, leaning against his chest. Golden hair with soft curls, her black eyes huge, and a plume of a tail that only tucked under when Blake came near, she wasn't exactly ugly, just skinny. "That dog's a star; she saved our lives, Gramps. You really think she's going back to the pound? She stays with us and will be loved and spoiled until she takes her last breath, right gang?"

The chorus of agreements was varied.

Kayla's came loud and clear, "Absolutely."

Angie's was a little more colorful and so was her face once she realized her words might be controversial. "Fucking A."

Blake was the last to respond, and got a resounding cheer for his vote. "If she lets me, I'll be *her* best friend, since what she did for us makes her ours. She stays. But only on one condition."

Everyone stopped breathing. He'd gotten their attention, big time.

"Since she's your star, you have to stay here and look after her, John. Besides, we need your calm, steadiness in our lives. Once I talk Charli into marrying me and we buy a bigger place, we'll be family. When that happens, we'll need the ultimate warrior who can keep us all in line."

Poppa John looked pleased, alarmed and thoughtful all at the same time. She could see multiple thoughts shifting in his head. Earlier statements he'd made came back to her. *Old people should live in homes, and let the young ones live their lives unencumbered by the worries of seniors and their problems.*

She took his hand, so he'd look into her eyes. "It's different with us, Popsicle, you know that. We all need you." Charli petted the furry head gently. "Star needs you."

"She has her name." John laughed when the dog added her persuasion by jumping up to lick his face, her teary, loving gaze almost as potent as Charli's. "Please, Gramps—"

"Alright, already. Don't beg. It would be my pleasure to stay here with you all." He wiped his eyes with his gnarled fingers, trying to hide the shakes.

Hugs and embraces followed and the uproar didn't settle down until they returned to their earlier conversation of what had taken place at the police station.

Kayla bragged, "I had Detective Newton—"

"He's Lieutenant Newton, Kayla." Blake interrupted.

"Even better. I got the bigshot to interview me." She beamed at everyone, and they all snickered. "He was really nice. Told me I was brave, and though he didn't agree with me having taken the firearm, since I'd used it to protect myself and everyone else, there'd be no charges."

Blake interrupted, "Speaking of taking firearms, how did you two know about my safe and the combination?"

Charli answered before the girls could, "They have a habit of listening at open doorways and heard your code."

Kayla looked away, her face red. But Angie just grinned.

"Right. I'll make sure it's changed." Blake added, "And close the doors before I reveal any more secrets."

Kayla started to apologize but stopped when Blake put his arm around her shoulders and pulled her close for a hug. "Don't ever apologize for today, Kayla. You did good, sweetheart, acting at the exact time you were needed."

"That's what the lieutenant said. I asked him about being a police officer, how his family felt about him being in danger sometimes, and he mentioned he had a daughter my age who'd asked him repeatedly to teach her how to use a gun, and he'd refused. He hated to think of her even near such a dangerous weapon. After what happened to us, he's rethinking his decision."

Blake cut in, "You go to the same school as Lisa, his daughter. She's a good kid. I'll introduce you two sometime."

Charli saw the slight withdrawal from Angie and squeezed Blake's knee where her hand had been resting while they sat with their chairs as close as possible. Not dumb, he picked up on it and added, "You too, Angie. You'll like Lisa, she's quiet and unassuming, but gets top marks in all her classes. Newton is damn proud of her and brags to the point of where I want to shove a roll of toilet paper in his mouth to stop it."

Laughing and brightening instantly, Angie nodded. Charli had noticed an extreme change in her new ward over the last two days. When she'd arrived with piercings in her eyebrows and multiple ones in her ears and lip, Charli had pretended not to be disturbed by anyone mutilating their body so savagely. Now that they'd been removed, she kind of missed the silver balls she'd previously gotten used to as part of the girl's identity.

Angie's hair, washed and tamed from the old style, now lay flat, an ordinary brown and lifeless, giving her the appearance of a stranger. Charli surmised the girl wanted to fit in to some stereotype she'd formed in her head.

They needed to have a talk. She'd soon let the girl know that she'd be loved no matter if she had a silver ring hanging off the end of her chin. If she liked her old image, she needed to keep it or find whatever suited her best.

She watched as Kayla reached over to take Angie's hand as her way of including her into their plans. As much as her heart went out to Angie's desperate need for stability, love and reassurance, Kayla had notched her own space in Charli's heart.

She'd proven to be an anomaly that needed to be researched carefully, with love and attention so the girl would bloom into her potential.

After the police had arrived at the scene earlier, Kayla had refused to let Charli go, as if she needed the reassurance of her arms and her soft voice telling her, "You did good, kiddo. We're fine, thanks to you. You're a hero now, baby."

It wasn't until she'd whispered the magic words that had Kayla pulling back so she could look into Charli's face. "I love you, too." Her response – a confession of such huge proportions that Charli knew she'd never said those words before.

After her grandfather had agreed to be a part of their newly formed family, they'd all joined in to clean up the dinner mess and separated to change into their swimming gear for late night family fun in the pool, a playful time of splashing, racing and diving, a wonderful release to the stress they'd been under.

The stars had provided a surprising light show and the warm evening air carried a lovely breeze that spread the fragrance of the surrounding tropical flowers. It swirled around to add a layer of detail to a night Charli would never forget.

She watched her grandfather swim carefully to the edge of the pool where the gradual stairs and a railing were there to help him get out. He scooped up Star, who'd waited impatiently for him to emerge, and held her close, his hand petting and calming.

Charli joined him there and listened as he spoke low. "It's been a wonderful night, kiddo, one of the best in a very long time."

"I'm glad, Popsicle. And I'm thrilled you agreed to stay with us. The girls need you just like I did when you brought me to live with you after Mom and Dad died."

"You were in so much pain; I wanted you to always know you weren't alone."

"You see, you're a genius, because I never felt that way. And now, Kayla and Angie will have the same good fortune of knowing that they belong because you'll be there to make sure."

He squeezed her hand. "For as long as I can stay with you, darling. Just know I'll try my damnedest not to kick the bucket too soon."

She giggled, like he wanted her to, but she also understood the warning as his way of reminding her his time with them would be limited. Even more reason not to waste a precious minute.

As she always did, she pushed the thoughts away and leaned her head on his shoulder. "Then we'll have to love you twice as hard while you're with us, won't we?"

They held hands as they sat on the stairs to watch Blake race Kayla and Angie from one end of the pool to the other, beating both, but having to work hard to outperform Kayla with her long legs and strong arms.

When Blake swam to the edge and pulled himself from the pool, his muscles glistening in the patio lights, Charli almost swallowed her tongue. The man's body exemplified that of a male model in a magazine sold to thrill women and spur on other men to work harder.

Every nerve in her body reacted. Not only for the pleasure she anticipated, but for the sheer need for them to have time alone. Everything had moved so fast, and though it all felt right, there were plans to be discussed and assurances made. And... a long honeymoon to enjoy.

One thing she did acknowledge. Any time she'd imagined joining into a relationship with a man, having a family, she'd had trouble picturing the scene. Everything inside her would scream, *are you out of your ever-loving mind?* Keep things simple, stupid. Live alone. Be yourself. Keep the doors locked between you and all that pain from the unknown.

Those thoughts were completely overshadowed now by her anticipation of life surrounded by people who loved each other. She couldn't make it happen fast enough.

Except for one thing... did Blake really know what he was letting himself in for?

Chapter
Fifty-six

Everyone else had settled down, the pool party ended, and finally Charli watched as Blake closed the door to their bedroom, shutting out the world.

He swept her into a hug, proving the last little while had been as hard for him as it had for her. "Alone at last! I love our family, but I couldn't wait to get you to myself."

"No kidding. The constant looks you were giving me were very revealing. They threatened all kinds of enjoyable compensations that had me on the edge most of the evening."

She kissed him with all the yearning he'd raised from those long, intent gazes and fleeting touches, the quick hugs and hands caressing her neck and hair. He'd seduced her with his eyes, and she'd loved the growing passion swirling around inside, with promises of a night to remember.

In seconds, his breathing turned harsh, his

hands began exploring and he deepened the kiss.

"Blake, we should discuss details—"

"No talk. I need to be inside you, our bodies joined the same way my heart's connected to yours. It's magic, baby. Pure spiritual. I've never felt like this before." As he talked, he helped her lose her swimsuit, and then chucked his own. Lifting her in his arms, her legs wrapped around his waist, arms around his neck, he carried her to the bed and lowered her. Leaning in so she could see his face, he stared into hers and stopped, looking his fill as she watched him memorize her features.

"What?"

"You're beautiful."

"Funny thing, I was thinking the same earlier about you."

He laughed. "Men aren't beautiful. They're too mundane and... and well... basic."

"And idiotic." She couldn't believe he had so little conceit. "Anyway, I wasn't just thinking of your body, silly, although that's a major turn-on. I was talking about that big old mushy heart you've kept hidden from all the other women in your life."

He appeared befuddled, endearingly so. "Do you realize if it wasn't for your grandfather, I'd be surrounded again? Even Star's a female. Thank God for John." He leaned in for a blistering kiss. Then he threaded his gentle fingers through her curls as he liked to do. "I have no doubt the good Lord will grace us with a family, and just to be persnickety, they'll be daughters as well."

She wriggled to remind him of his earlier intentions and grinned when she saw his interest flare.

Interpreting the hint, he slipped inside her and loved her so well that afterwards she lay gasping, sweating and totally drained... fulfilled.

In love.

She lay next to him, listening to his heavy breathing, and knew he'd had the same breathtaking experience that had rocked her world.

She heard over and over his declarations of love while his body proved what his heart felt and his lips whispered.

Her thoughts meandered to the future, her new family all together under one roof, loving each other, sharing... her Poppa John living with them, giving them the benefit of his wisdom. The girls growing, learning, developing into strong adults under their guidance and loving help.

Blake and her – a couple – working together to become a solid unit. A new home, one to accommodate everyone, plus a nursery, and a yard for Star.

She could see their wedding now. Blake as handsome as sin in a typical black tux. Her in a white silky gown, long swirling skirt, red roses in her bouquet, her grandmother's pearls at her throat and her mother's veil... tucked into her *red curls.*

Afterword

Thank you so much for reading my book,
Special Agent Charli

I absolutely loved writing this story and I hope you enjoyed reading it. If so, I would ask you for a favor. Wherever you purchased this book, please take a few minutes and leave an honest review. _I would love to know your sentiments about the character called Poppa John – you just have to know I'll read every single comment… xo_

Authors enjoy hearing that readers like their stories, and hopefully, others will see your words and choose to buy my work because of your kind sentiments.

My website at **http://mimibarbour.com** now has all my books listed with links to the venues to make it easy for you to return to where you bought the book and to find my other work.

While you're there, I'd really appreciate it if you would sign up for my newsletter so I can keep in touch. **http://bit.ly/mimibarbournewsletter** I only send out newsletters approximately twice a month. It's usually full of giveaways, contests and freebies along with my personal news. (You have my word that your address will never be shared.)

Poppa John's Christmas Village

Of course, I had to use it for a book cover, didn't
I? He was so proud...

Meet, Poppa John

Hugs, Mimi

Special Agent Booker

Undercover FBI

Book #5
by
NYT & USA Today, best-selling author,
Mimi Barbour

~*~*~

Suspense lights up in every page of this fast-paced

blockbuster of thrills!

When Sloan Booker's father dies tragically, he has no other option but to give up his job as an FBI agent and take over his family's vehicle restoration business in Oahu, Hawaii. Giving up his badge is difficult but having Homeland Security and his old boss request the use of his house in a stakeout, spying on his Muslim neighbors who they suspect are terrorists, is just too damn much for a man already frazzled. It makes no difference that they've offered him a partner to be in charge of the surveillance... until he meets the gorgeous divorcee.

Special Agent Alia Hawkins might look more like a model than a cop but looks can be deceiving. Not only does she rescue street kids, fights their battles and transports them to safe homes, but since she lived many years in Pakistan and speaks their language, she's a sought after agent. So far, she's kept her personal life and job separate. But when Alia's slimy ex-husband threatens to steal her eight-year-old son, she has no choice but to bring the kid along on her latest undercover assignment – living with a hotshot, sexy as hell agent under the guise of his long lost stepsister. Her life suddenly takes some drastic swerves and she wonders if things will ever slow down.

Praise:

"A very enjoyable story. Loved reading about Sloan Booker and his temporary partner, Alia. Their chemistry is unmatched, and the case they are working on made for a fun read that was hard to put down. Since each book in this series is a standalone, you can also read them in any order without being lost at all."
Reviewed by ~ Laura

"This author's writing style is so sharp you can hear it snap. The story is engrossing and highly entertaining. The characters are interesting and they face many twists and turns along the way in this suspenseful read. The pace steadily builds to an exciting conclusion. Excellent read!"
Reviewed by ~ DJ Faz

"I loved this one. There was so much action and suspense, and I connected instant with all of the characters. I also liked the surprise at the end. The story line flowed beautifully with numerous issues. I WANT BOOK #6!"
Reviewed by ~ AZ Csutomer

Chapter One – Special Agent Booker

Alia scoured the dark parking lot behind the Ilikia Hotel looking for the boy. Palm trees and plumeria decorated the area, but there was no sign of a kid in trouble.

Ruby had sworn he'd be here, and woken from a dead sleep at three a.m. to jump in to her jeans and then drive like a maniac to get to him in time, Alia hadn't stopped to ask a lot of questions.

Now she called Ruby using her hands-free in the car. "He's not here. Did he call you back?"

"His name is Justin, and no, I haven't heard from him. He said he'd gotten away from his player; that the guy had roughed him up. He hid out at the Ilikia and another dude came on to him. Scared stupid, he called me, told me he was behind the dumpster."

"Okay, I'll check it out."

Alia pulled the car over, got out and headed in that direction. As she approached, she saw a man bending over something wedged in between two dumpsters. "Listen, kid, I don't want to hurt you. Come out and I'll buy you something to eat. We'll talk. You can stay in my room so you'll have a place to sleep."

"Leave me alone. I'm not going anywhere with you." The boy's voice cracked, his tone going from soprano to bass in one sentence.

"Hey, is that any way to act with someone who just wants to help? I'm being nice, but I can—"

"Be a lying prick who wants to get you alone and do nasty things to you. He knows, don't you, Justin?" Alia stood waiting, hoping her insults would piss the scumbag off enough he'd come at her. Then she could kick the shit out of the perverted prick.

Tall, with a kangaroo pouch of sloppy fat in front, the guy shot to his feet as if she'd shoved a stick up his ass. "What the fuck! Who the hell are you?"

"I'm Justin's friend. And I have a real aversion to

pedophiles. Actually, I like to arrest the scum, book 'em and hope they never get another moment of freedom to do those icky things they like to do."

The troll looked her up and down and foolishly decided it was no contest. His fist punched air as she dropped in defense and drove her own up into his groin area. Rolling to the side and then to her feet in the nimble way she'd been trained, she tackled the bent-over screamer and pushed him into the steel side of the dumpster. Then she left her fist imprinted on his balls yet again. About this time, Justin slid out of his hidey-hole to level a kick into the guy's ribs for his personal parting shot.

"Enough, kid. Let's go. He'll have some healing to do. Hope it ruins the bastard's Hawaiian holiday."

She ran back to her SUV, and Justin followed. Once in the car, she checked him out. The kid was scrawny with a feminine delicacy many young girls would get surgery to have. His features were ethereal: lovely eyes that looked to be a pale color in the car's dimness, and thick blond hair that hung to his scrawny shoulders curled in ringlets. Justin might have been born a boy, but no doubt he'd pull in top dollar for any pimp who played him right.

"I'm taking you to a safe home, okay? You called Ruby, and that's the way this works. They'll help you. If you want a new start, they'll make it happen."

Slouched in the corner, tears pouring, the youngster sniffed. He looked at her, those big eyes begging not to be judged, and she reached over, her hand open and waiting. Though hardened to some degree by what she'd seen in the past, she still cared about these kids she saved, or she'd have stopped taking the calls.

His hand grasped hers and clung. "Thank you for what you did back there. Even if you are a cop."

"I'm actually a federal agent, and it was my pleasure. Truly!" She tightened her hand around his and shook it. "I lie... not. It *was* my pleasure." She grinned and waited, taking her eyes from the road for a second.

His fingers squeezed hers tight. "You have no idea what it meant to me seeing you there tonight. No one's ever saved me before."

"Hey, Justin. When you kids call Ruby, either I, or someone like me, will come. It's as simple as that."

If you liked the beginning of this story, and you want to read the rest, you'll find it on AMAZON.

Sweet Retaliation

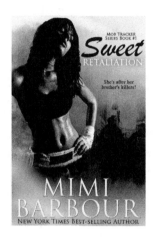

Mob Tracker Series

Book #1
by
Mimi Barbour
NYT & USA Today Best-selling author

*** *Warning: This is a series that must be read in order!!*

A virgin librarian with hot-chick potential, the conflicts in her story won't let you put the book down. Be prepared for an all-nighter...

She watches the mob kill her twin and is too frozen with fear to stop them. How can she live with that cowardice eating away at her self-respect? Revenge claws at her sheltered existence until she can't breathe. Though she's naïve, she isn't stupid. When she finds a stash of loot in her brother's gym locker, she has the means.

Now all she needs is the guts to make every one of those low-life gang members pay.

People might think detectives are hard-assed cops with no home life, but Trace McGuire has a dying mom he loves fiercely. Already stressed over his personal problems, he takes a bullet for a virgin beauty hiding while mobsters shoot her brother.

This chick draws out every protective instinct he thought had disintegrated over years on the job and he becomes invested – in her hot body, her plans for retaliation and her fighting spirit.

Helpless, he watches her enter the seedy underworld that'll eat her alive.

Then he sees her fight.

And wonders if they'll survive her.

Praise:

"I am in love with this book and I'll be following the series for more! Mimi Barbour did an awesome job!" ~ *Reviewed by Birna Bjornsdottir*

"Trace – oh Trace how I love you! As soon as he appeared in the story I knew I would fall in love with him and I did! He was a really great character, independent, focused and not afraid to push the limits when needed. Together he and Cass were amazing!

I really cannot wait to read more from this author in the future and highly recommend this story! You will have a hard time putting it down once you have started!" ~ *Reviewed by Katie_83*

"Ms. Barbour has written a gripping story about one woman's quest for justice. She has deftly created marvelous characters that pull you into their story. This is a suspense-filled, full-bore non-stop action ride that you will absolutely love." ~ *Reviewed by Colorado Avid Reader*

About the author, Mimi Barbour

MIMI BARBOUR: New York Times & USA Today Best-selling, award-winning romance author has written seven series, many single tiles and is involved in a huge number of box collections.

She lives on the beautiful East coast of Vancouver Island and writes her books with tongue-in-cheek and a mad glint in her eye. The fans all agree that it's the fascinating characters she creates which makes her writing so entertaining and brings them back for more of her magic.

"The favorite part of my job is meeting the characters from each new book. Designing them the way I want and having them act however I think they should. It's thrilling, especially when most of my make-believe folks are people I would love to interact with in reality."

Contact me

Amazon author page: http://bit.ly/
MimiBarbourAmazon

My website: http://www.mimibarbour.com/

Or follow me on twitter: https://twitter.com/
MimiBarbour

Or on Facebook: Mimi Barbour Fan page

Please sign up for my fun Newsletter: http://bit.ly/
mimibarbournewsletter

or

Write to me anytime. I love to hear from my
readers xo
mailto:mimibarbour66@gmail.com

Printed in Great Britain
by Amazon